Know Your baby lock

Know Your baby lock

by Naomi Baker and Tammy Young

Chilton Book Company

Radnor, Pennsylvania

Copyright © 1990 by Naomi Baker
and Tammy Young

Published in Radnor, Pennsylvania
19089, by Chilton Book Company

Cover Design by Tony Jacobson
Designed by Martha Vercoutere
Color Photographs by Lee Phillips
Illustrations by Chris Hansen

Manufactured in the United States of
America

Library of Congress Cataloging in
Publication Data

Baker, Naomi
    Know your baby lock / Naomi
    Baker and Tammy Young.

        p. cm.—(Creative machine arts
    series)
    Includes index.
    1. Serging 2. Sewing machines.
I. Young, Tammy. II. Title. III. Series.
TT713.B3324 1990   90-55324
646.2'044—dc20   CIP
ISBN 0-8019-8106-9 (pbk.)

3 4 5 6 7 8 9 0   9 8 7 6 5 4 3 2

Contents

Preface

A little over a decade ago, sergers (or as they're sometimes called, overlock machines) appeared on the home-sewing market. Most sergers at that time were industrial models—big, noisy, difficult to operate, with dangerous knives, and always breaking down.

But home-sewing serger models were a very different piece of equipment than their industrial cousins. They've been domesticated, with practically all the advantages and few of the drawbacks.

Small, clean, quiet, and safe, sergers now give us creative possibilities that previously were not available to the home-sewer. During the last decade, enthusiasts have taken serger sewing from a few basic stitches and techniques to a wide variety of decorative applications and innovative uses. We call the latest developments in decorative serger sewing **ornamental serging**.

As the publisher and consulting editor of the *Serger Update* newsletter and co-authors of two books on serging published by Chilton Book Company, we have been in a unique position to witness firsthand the exciting developments in the art of serger sewing. New equipment, technology, and notions have opened up more and more possibilities for creativity.

Tacony Corporation, the manufacturer of *baby lock* sergers, has been a leader in the advancement of these creative serging developments. Tacony has strongly promoted education and experimentation, leading to new ornamental serging possibilities.

Know Your baby lock is meant to encourage you to join this exciting pioneering effort, taking you beyond the basics and encouraging you to explore uses for the serger as an artistic instrument. We outline methods for seaming, edge-finishing, binding and trimming, and other decorative serging techniques. Simple projects are included at the end of every lesson to demonstrate skills. These projects are excellent for quick gifts, as well as for hands-on teaching.

We hope this book will encourage you to join the world of ornamental serging. Your handy *baby lock* will execute the basics beautifully. But taken one step further, it can easily make all of your serging projects one-of-a-kind creations.

So breeze through the basics (if you haven't already), and begin to look at all the creative serging options.

Happy ornamental serging,

Naomi Baker and Tammy Young

Foreword

Those of us lucky enough to own a serger need no convincing that as an invention, it ranks right up there with Post-it Notes, rotary cutters, and the microwave.

Yet those of us brave enough to tell the whole truth will confess that we've barely scratched the surface of our serger's capabilities.

I'm no different. Though I'm devoted to my serger, I've used it primarily to clean finish seam allowances. I'd like to do more, but my time for experimenting is limited. What I need is a master teacher at my side, coaxing me to twirl those knobs, change that thread, try this technique.

Shazam! Not one, but two master teachers have appeared through a puff of smoke. Tammy and Naomi, in the pages of this book, are exactly what you and I need. They walk us through the basics, and then lesson by lesson, teach a new technique, ending with a sample project using that technique. Some of my favorite ornamental serging techniques are the serged frog closure, elastic button loops, and double-bound seams.

For a busy sewer, this lesson format is ideal. You can try a lesson in an evening, make a sample for your notebook, then choose your favorite techniques to embellish a garment on the weekend.

By the time you finish, you will truly know your serger.

Robbie Fanning

Series Editor

Are you interested in a quarterly newsletter about creative uses of the sewing machine, serger, and knitting machine? Write to The Creative Machine-bl , PO Box 2634, Menlo Park, CA 94026.

Acknowledgments

This book would not have been possible without the full cooperation and assistance of Tacony Corporation, the manufacturer of *baby lock* sergers. Special thanks to Cheryl Robinson, the Tacony educational staff, and the entire company management for their enthusiastic support.

Our professional *Serger Update* writing team also helped give us the background for numerous creative ideas and techniques. A big thanks to Gail Brown, Anne Marie Soto, Jan Saunders, Nancy Nix-Rice, and Sue Green for their inspiration.

Several industry professionals have also contributed significantly to our background of creative serging applications. We want to thank Ervena Yu, Jon Harris, and Patsy Shields for introducing us to ideas developed in this book.

We also want to thank the talented people who have helped us immeasurably in producing the book: Chris Hansen, illustration; Lee Phillips, photography; Martha Vercoutere, book design; and Lori Bottom, manuscript preparation.

Finally, many thanks go to our editor, Robbie Fanning, and our publisher's representative, Kathryn Conover, for believing in our efforts and encouraging us to write the first brand-specific book on ornamental serging techniques.

The following are registered trademark names used in this book: *baby lock, Candlelight, Decor 6, Fray Check, Lycra, Perfect Pleater, Ripstop, Seams Great, Stiffy, TAC Spray Stiff, Teflon, Thinsulate, Ultrasuede, Velcro,* and *Wonder-Under.*

1. baby lock Basics

- Bonding with Your Serger
- Serging and Sewing Strategies
- How to Use this Book
- *baby lock* Features
- *baby lock* Stitch Formation
- *baby lock* Feet and Accessories
- Loving Care

Bonding with Your Serger

The biggest hurdle to overcome in the exciting adventure of serger sewing is **taking the machine out of the box**. Yes, that's right! Over the years, we've found that for many home-sewers, thc scrger looked wonderful when demonstrated in the store. It was capable of speedy seaming, pretty rolled edges, and all sorts of decorative techniques. But when the home-sewer brought it home, the serger seemed daunting and complicated. (After all, it's an entirely different kind of machine than the sewing machine we all have known.) So into the closet it goes, just waiting for that rainy day when there's plenty of time to figure it out and to practice all of those wonderful serger techniques.

Of course, the longer the serger stays in the closet, the more complex and intimidating it seems. Meanwhile, your "friendly" sewing machine is right there to fall back on.

The next hurdle in serger use occurs when we do take the machine out of the box, and the dealer has adjusted it for a perfectly balanced seam. We can serge beautifully balanced seams and edges, but heaven forbid that we might have to switch to a rolled edge or a flatlock. Horrors! That might involve taking out a needle, removing a stitch finger, changing a plate, or adjusting the tension settings. The thought of tackling all these separate steps seems overwhelming at first.

But just stop and consider how many different adjustments you make effortlessly on your sewing machine—winding the bobbin, threading, changing needles and feet, making stitch-length adjustments, and converting to special stitches. The serger only seems complicated at first, when we're getting used to it and to its unique method of sewing.

There's a simple answer. Take your serger out of the box, read the owner's instruction manual, and practice the various kinds of stitches available on your model. In other words, **use your serger and you'll become comfortable with it sooner than you think.**

Serger expert Sue Green calls this process "bonding." Although the term is most often used for parents' feeling toward their child or for other personal relationships, it applies nicely to serger-sewing as well. As you spend more time with your machine and get to know it, you'll learn its idiosyncrasies, talents, and personality. At varying times this bonding process can be frustrating, exciting, intimidating, or rewarding—and just plain fun. Sharpening your spirit of adventure can be a big help.

If serging classes are available to you, by all means take advantage of them. They're a great way to speed up the learning process, pick up tips and techniques, and have a good time in the process.

In this book, we assume that you have already learned the basics of serger sewing. Check the following list to be sure.

____ Threading
____ Changing and balancing tension
____ Changing stitch width and length
____ Adjusting for a rolled edge—a simple procedure on the *baby lock*. Practice until you can do it effortlessly.
____ Adjusting for 2-thread serging
____ Adjusting for 2- and 3-thread flatlocking
____ Using the differential feed
____ Changing needles
____ Cleaning your machine, and oiling it (only if necessary)
____ Clearing the stitch finger
____ Serging inside and outside corners
____ Ripping out stitches

Your instruction manual is a must. If you don't have one, buy or order one from your dealer. The manual contains detailed instructions on the basics listed above. Work your way through the manual early in your bonding process.

In addition to your manual, several excellent books are available to lead you through all the machine basics and construction techniques and beyond. (See the listing under Other Publications by the Authors, page 176.) For the more recent *baby lock* models, an owner's workbook and instructional video are also available.

When sergers were first introduced in the United States, their use was limited to simple seams and edges. Since then, serger sewing enthusiasts have developed a great deal of exciting new information. As you get to know your serger and put it to work, you'll discover a whole new world of ornamental serging possibilities.

Serging and Sewing Strategies

Your serger is a natural companion to your sewing machine. Rather than working in competition with each other, these two machines team up to offer us endless possibilities. Once you're familiar with your serger and all its potential uses, you'll learn to decide between using your sewing machine or your serger for any project or parts of a project.

The serger is fast, finishes edges beautifully, makes neat, sturdy seams, and replicates many of the looks found in today's ready-to-wear. It efficiently sews many specialty fabrics we would have hesitated to tackle in the past, including sheers, silkies, and loosely wovens. The built-in stretch of a serger stitch also makes serging a favored option for interlocks, *Lycra* blends, and sweatering.

We've often heard that the serger speeds up sewing, that it trims, seams, and overlocks in one step, that it makes beautiful rolled edges and has many decorative uses. But the one thing we don't always hear is that **serger sewing is all about edges**. (Fig. 1-1)

Because the loopers must go above and below the fabric in order to form an overlock stitch, most serging must necessarily be done on edges or folds. One exception is a double chain stitch formed by the needle and lower looper (available only on the BL4-625, BL4-605, and EA-605 models).

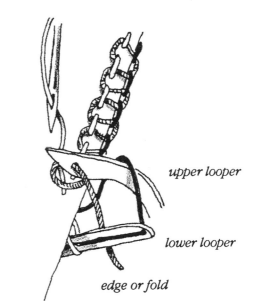

upper looper

lower looper

edge or fold

Fig. 1-1: *Because of a serger's looper mechanism, serging is always placed on an edge or fold.*

The serger's ability to sew on edges includes seams (see Chapter 3), flatlocking (in Lesson 3 and Lesson 25), and edge finishing (discussed in Chapter 4). Beyond these basics, interesting variations abound.

The sewing machine, unlike the serger, has the ability to sew anywhere on a piece of fabric, not just on an edge or fold. Its straight-stitch capability—for top-stitching and edge-stitching—is essential for many serger techniques. And its decorative stitches can be combined with serging to enhance your creativity.

Plan each of your sewing projects (whether garments, accessories, or home decorating items) in advance. Where can you add ornamental details for the most artistic and pleasing results? Consider possibilities for seams and edges. Consider decorative flatlocking. What are your other options? (Fig. 1-2)

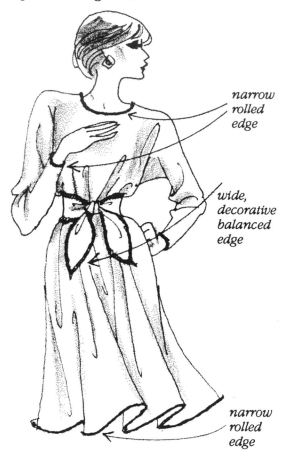

narrow rolled edge

wide, decorative balanced edge

narrow rolled edge

Fig. 1-2: *Plan your serging projects with decorative detail in mind.*

Experiment, then give it your best shot. But remember, subtlety can often be more pleasing than overdoing it, so don't try to decorate every edge or seam on any one project. Choose those areas where your ornamental serging will be the most effective.

The lessons and projects throughout this book are just a beginning. Once you understand the basics of serger sewing, you too can become a serger artist. It's simply a matter of focus and awareness. Ornamental serging can be applied to even the simplest T-shirt to make it look like designer sportswear (see page 56).

Practice, experimentation, failure, and success are all part of the process. So accept the challenge and join us in the latest phase of serger sewing—ornamental serging.

How to Use this Book

Know Your baby lock has been designed to lead you quickly through the basics (Chapters 1 and 2) and into the fun world of ornamental serging. You'll find 38 lessons, grouped into chapters on seams, edges, trims and bindings, special techniques, serged closures, and artistic possibilities.

The lessons take you from decorative basics to more advanced skills. A simple project is included at the end of every lesson so you can easily practice the techniques you have learned.

Less experienced serger users may want to follow the lessons numerically to learn basic skills before moving on to advanced ones. If you come to a term you don't understand, refer to the Glossary of Serging Terms on page 169. Experienced seamsters can easily skip around in the book, choosing to study a lesson when it applies to a current project.

Regardless of your level of experience, the Table of Contents can help you decide quickly which decorative seams, edges, bindings, or other techniques to use for any serger project. When you've mastered all of the lessons in *Know Your baby lock*, you'll feel comfortable selecting even the most advanced ornamental serging applications.

baby lock Features

The *baby lock* is an ideal machine for ornamental serging. Its renowned rolled edges, even on early models, are clean and crisp. Many *baby lock* models have multiple stitch options with easy width and length adjustments. The newest *baby lock* models (BL4-838D and BL5380ED) feature two-speed electronic foot control and built-in needle and lower looper threaders. But regardless of the model, your *baby lock* offers many artistic possibilities.

In addition to *baby lock* sergers , Tacony has also introduced a new blindstitch machine—model BL101. (Fig. 1-3) This machine is ideal for

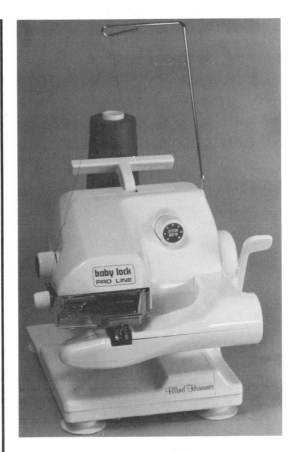

Fig. 1-3: *The new* baby lock *blindhem machine (model #BL101) combines serger and sewing machine technology.*

both professionals and active home-sewers. It forms perfect blindhems by using a looper system (like a serger) rather than a bobbin system (like a sewing machine). However, it does not trim and overcast like a serger. The BL101 is essentially the home version of an industrial machine, combining the latest technologies of sewing machines and sergers.

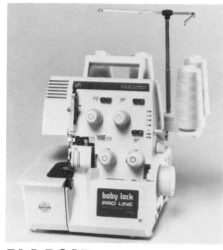

BL4-B38D

BL5380ED

A baby lock
Photo Gallery

BL4-738

BL5280E

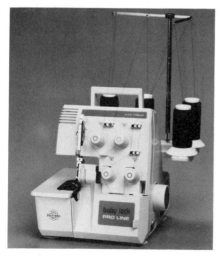

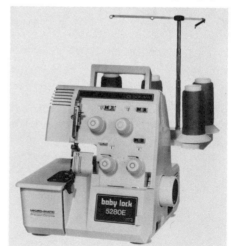

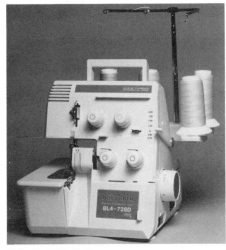

BL4-728D

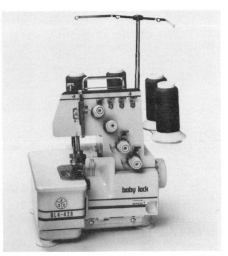

BL4-428

BL3-437

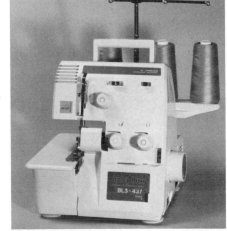

BL3-416

BL4-605

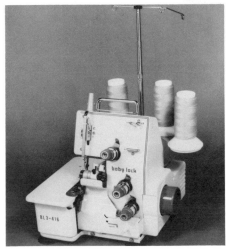

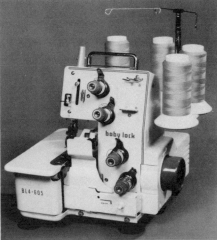

baby lock Features

	BL4-838D	BL5380ED	BL4-738 BL4-738D	BL5280E BL5280ED	BL4-728 BL4-728D	BL4-736 BL4-736D	BL5260 BL5260D	BL4-428	BL5180
4-thread overedge	yes		yes		yes	yes		yes	
4-thread mock safety		yes		yes			yes		yes
4-thread safety									
3-thread overlock	yes	yes	yes	yes	yes	yes	yes	yes	yes
2-thread overedge	yes	yes	yes	yes	yes	yes	yes	yes	yes
2-thread double chain									
# of needles	2	2	2	2	2	2	2	2	2
needle	DCX1F	DCX1F	DCX1F	DCX1F	DCX1F	DCX1F	DCX1F	DCX1F	DCX1F
stitch width capacity	3.5mm to 7.5mm	3.5mm to 7.5mm	3.5mm to 7.5mm	3.5mm to 7.5mm	3.5mm to 7.5mm	4.0mm to 6.2mm	4.0mm to 6.2mm	2.5mm to 7.5mm	2.5mm to 7.5mm
stitch width adjustment	dial	dial	dial	dial	adjust knife	remove left or right needle	remove left needle	dial	dial
stitch length adjustment	push button	push button	push button	push button	push button	push button	push button	push button	push button
rolled hem adjustment	built-in	built-in	built-in	built-in	built-in	change plate (included)	change plate (included)	built-in	built-in
self-threading lower looper	yes	yes	yes	yes	yes	yes	yes	yes	yes
snap-on presser foot	yes	yes	yes	yes	yes	on 736D	on 5260D	n/a	yes
tension type	numbered multiple revolution	numbered multiple revolution	numbered multiple revolution	numbered multiple revolution	numbered single revolution	numbered single revolution	numbered single revolution	numbered multiple revolution	numbered multiple revolution
elastic/tape guide	built into presser foot	built into presser foot	built into presser foot	built into presser foot	built into presser foot	n/a	n/a	built into presser foot	built into presser foot

baby lock Features

	BL4-436 BL4-436D BL4-714	BL3200 BL3-418	BL3-408	BL3-437	BL3-417 BL3-407	BL3-426	BL3-416 BL3-406 BL3-318	BL4-625 BL4-605 EA-605	
4-thread overedge	yes								
4-thread mock safety									
4-thread safety								yes	
3-thread overlock	yes	yes	yes	yes	yes	yes	yes		
2-thread overedge		yes	yes	no	yes	no	no	yes	
2-thread double chain								yes	
# of needles	2	1	1	1	1	1	1	2	
needle	DCX1F	DCX1	DCX1	DCX1F	DCX1	DCX1	DCX1	BLX2N	
stitch width capacity	4.0mm to 6.2mm	2.5mm to 5.3mm	2.5mm to 5.3mm	3.8mm	2.5mm to 5.0mm	2.5mm to 5.0mm	2.5mm to 5.0mm	4.0mm to 7.0mm	
stitch width adjustment	remove left or right needle	dial	dial	n/a	manual	manual	manual	n/a	
stitch length adjustment	push button	push button	manual	push button	manual	push button	manual	push button	
rolled hem adjustment	change plate (included)	built in	built in	change plate (included)	change plate (included)	change plate	change plate	n/a	
self-threading lower looper	n/a	yes	n/a	yes	n/a	n/a	n/a	n/a	
snap-on presser foot	n/a	n/a	n/a	n/a	n/a	n/a	n/a	n/a	
tension type	multiple revolution	multiple revolution	multiple revolution	numbered single revolution	multiple revolution	multiple revolution	multiple revolution	multiple revolution	
elastic/tape guide	n/a	n/a	n/a	n/a	n/a	n/a	n/a	n/a	

baby lock Features

	BL4-838D	BL5380ED	BL4-738 BL4-738D	BL5280E BL5280ED	BL4-728 BL4-728D	BL4-736 BL4-736D	BL5260 BL5260D	BL4-428	BL5180
built-in thread cutter	yes	yes	yes	yes	n/a	n/a	n/a	n/a	n/a
accessory storage	yes	yes	yes	yes	no	no	no	no	no
2-thread flatlock	yes	yes	yes	yes	yes	yes	yes	yes	yes
2-thread blindhem	yes	yes	yes	yes	yes	yes	yes	yes	yes
differential feed	yes	yes	on 738D	on 5280ED	on 728D	on 736D	on 5260D	n/a	n/a
2-thread conversion	built-in	built-in	built-in	built-in	manual	manual	manual	built-in	built-in
built-in light	yes	yes	yes	yes	yes	yes	yes	yes	yes
maximum sewing speed	1500	1500	1500	1500	1500	1500	1500	1500	1500
knife disengages	yes	yes	yes	yes	yes	yes	yes	yes	yes
stitch length	1–4mm	1–4mm	738D/1–4mm 738/1–5mm	5280ED/ 1–4mm 5280E/1–5mm	728D/1–4mm 728/1–5mm	736D/1–4mm 736/1–5mm	5260D/1–4mm 5260/1–5mm	1–5mm	1–5mm
accessories included	packet A	packet A	packet A	packet A	packet B	packet D	packet D	packet E	packet E
optional blindhem foot	yes	yes	yes	yes	yes	yes	yes	yes	yes
optional ornamental stitch guide	yes	yes	yes	yes	yes	yes	yes	yes	yes
instructional video tape	yes	yes	yes	yes	yes	yes	yes	yes	yes
owner's workbook	yes	yes	yes	yes	yes	yes	yes	no	no

baby lock Features

	BL4-436 BL4-436D BL4-714	BL3200 BL3-418	BL3-408	BL3-437	BL3-417 BL3-407	BL3-426	BL3-416 BL3-406 BL3-318	BL4-625 BL4-605 EA-605	
built-in thread cutter	n/a	n/a	n/a	n/a	n/a	n/a	n/a	n/a	
accessory storage	n/a	n/a	n/a	n/a	n/a	n/a	n/a	n/a	
2-thread flatlock	n/a	yes	yes	n/a	yes	n/a	n/a	yes	
2-thread blindhem	n/a	yes	yes	n/a	yes	n/a	n/a	yes	
differential feed	on 436D	n/a	n/a	n/a	n/a	n/a	n/a	n/a	
2-thread conversion	n/a	built-in	built-in	n/a	built-in	n/a	n/a	n/a	
built-in light	yes	yes	n/a	yes	on 417	yes	n/a	only on 625	
maximum sewing speed	1500	1500	1500	1500	1500	1500	1500	1500	
knife disengages	yes	yes	yes	yes	yes	yes	yes	yes	
stitch length	436D/1–4mm 436/1–5mm 714/1–5mm	1–5mm	1–5mm	1–5mm	1–5mm	1–5mm	1–5mm	1–5mm	
accessories included	packet F	packet J	packet G	see below	packet I	packet I	packet I	packet C	
optional blindhem foot	yes	yes	yes	yes	yes	yes	yes	no	
optional ornamental stitch guide	yes	yes	yes	yes	yes	yes	yes	yes	
instructional video tape	n/a	yes	yes	n/a	n/a	n/a	n/a	n/a	
owner's workbook	n/a	n/a	n/a	n/a	n/a	n/a	n/a	n/a	

baby lock
Stitch Formation

Every model of serger has one or more stitch options. Refer to the chart on page 8 or to your manual to determine the stitches available on your model. If this book is your own, use a highlighter pen to mark your machine's features.

4-thread overedge stitch
(Fig. 1-4)

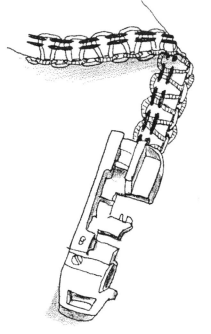

Fig. 1-4: *Stitch formation—4-thread overedge.*

■ Sometimes referred to as a 3/4-thread overlock stitch.

■ The upper looper interlocks with the left needle, so all four threads interlock.

■ Durable for seaming and decorative finishing (up to 7.5mm wide) and fully stretchable.

■ Converts to a 3-thread overlock stitch by removing either needle. Use the left needle for a wide stitch and the right needle for a narrow stitch.

■ Converts to a 2-thread overedge stitch, using the lower looper and either needle.

4-thread mock safety stitch
(Fig. 1-5)

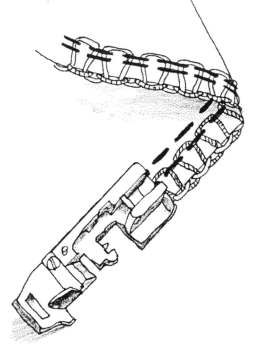

Fig. 1-5: *Stitch formation—4-thread mock safety stitch.*

■ Sometimes referred to as a variation of the 3/4-thread overlock stitch.

- A comparable option to the 4-thread overedge stitch above (they're never both available on the same machine).

- The upper looper interlocks with the right needle (but not the left needle).

- Converts to a narrow, 3-thread overlock or 2-thread overedge stitch by removing the left needle. Will not form a wide 2- or 3-thread stitch with the left needle.

- Durable and stretchable for seaming and decorative finishing

4-thread safety stitch
(Fig. 1-6)

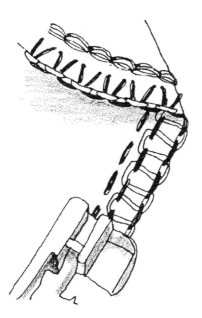

Fig. 1-6: Stitch formation—4-thread safety stitch.

- Often called a 4/2-thread stitch.

- A combination of a double chainstitch and a 2-thread overedge stitch. Essentially, a chainstitched seam with a finished edge.

- The stitch can be converted to chain only or to the overedge only.

- Durable and stable. Used for loosely woven fabrics and to stabilize stretchy areas.

3-thread overlock stitch
(Fig. 1-7)

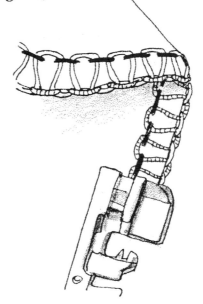

Fig. 1-7: Stitch formation—3-thread overlock.

- Threads interlock at the seamline to form a stretchable, yet durable, seam or edge finish.

- Available on most *baby lock* models.

2-thread overedge stitch
(Fig. 1-8)

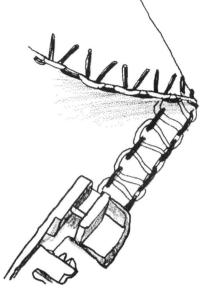

Fig. 1-8: Stitch formation—2-thread overedge.

■ Threads do not lock at the seamline.

■ Less bulky than 3- or 4-thread stitching.

■ Used for decorative or lightweight edge finishing, flatlocking, or flatlock seaming. Doesn't form a (more stable) locking seam.

Double chainstitch
(Fig. 1-9)

■ A needle thread forms a straight stitch on the top of the fabric, and a looper thread interlocks to form a chain on the underside (available on only three *baby lock* models).

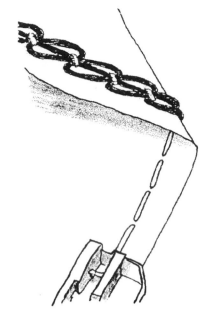

Fig. 1-9: Stitch formation—double chainstitch.

■ A secure stitch with little or no stretch.

■ Used for top-stitching (with the chain on top), seaming, or hemming.

baby lock Feet and Accessories

Many *baby lock* models have special feet and accessories to make ornamental serging easier. Refer to the *baby lock* features chart on page 8 or your manual to determine the specific options on your machine.

Elastic/tape guide (Fig. 1-10)— Top-of-the-line *baby lock* models have an elastic/tape guide built into the standard presser foot. When you serge over filler (thread, cord, ribbon, yarn, fishline, or wire), you can use this handy feature to guide the filler into position.

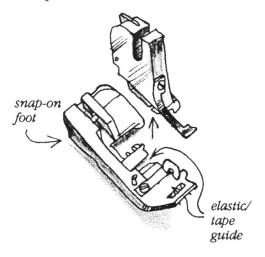

snap-on foot

elastic/ tape guide

Fig. 1-10: *Standard foot on top-of-the-line* baby lock *models.*

Snap-on feet—Several *baby lock* models feature snap-on presser feet for ease in changing to and from an optional foot.

In most cases, the optional foot will be the blindhem foot (see opposite). The snap-on feet also allow easy access for threading and changing needles.

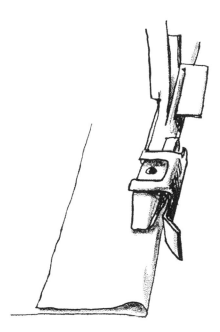

Fig. 1-11: *The blindhem foot accurately guides stitching along a fold—ideal for flatlocking and blind hems.*

Blindhem foot (Fig. 1-11)—This handy optional foot fits all current *baby lock* models except those with a 4-thread safety stitch. In addition to blind hemming (instructions are included with the foot), this foot is ideal for accurately guiding serger stitching along a fold. For specific uses, see perfecting flatlocking (Lessons 3 and 25), serger lace (Lesson 24), and serge-picked zippers (Lesson 32).

Other specialty feet—As we finished this book, we learned that Tacony plans to introduce an elastic foot. Other specialty feet are also on the

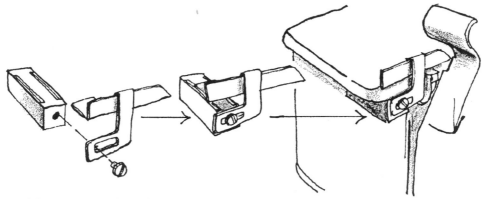

Fig. 1-12: *The ornamental stitching guide also helps guide stitching.*

drawing board. Because of rapid technological advancements, check with your dealer regularly. After all, if you're using your serger for creative, ornamental purposes, you won't want to miss out on the latest developments.

Ornamental stitching guide (Fig. 1-12) —This guide is another useful accessory that fits all *baby lock* models. It magnetically attaches and screws into place on the bed of the serger, as shown, to help guide your serging, much as a blindhem foot does. For some models, an adapter strip must be purchased along with the guide so that it will adhere properly to the bed.

Standard baby lock accessories—All *baby lock* sergers come with a packet of useful accessories. When you purchase any model, you'll receive one or two screwdrivers, a package of needles, a lower-knife replacement blade, tweezers, a lint brush, spool caps, and thread nets (refer to your manual for instructions). With most models, you'll also receive a vinyl cover to keep your machine dust-free when it's not in use. With some models, other machine-specific accessories (such as a convert looper, a needleplate, an oiler, or a heart-shaped driver for adjusting stitch length) are included, too. Refer to your manual for detailed information.

Loving Care

Your serger is a precision instrument. If you treat it well, it will reward you with years of ornamental serging. But without proper care, it can create problems on even the simplest project.

You may not be taking your sewing machine in for regular checkups, but for your serger regular checkups are essential. The serger's timing and accuracy need to be much more finely tuned than the sewing machine's.

Follow the basic guidelines on the next page (Fig. 1-13) to keep your serger running smoothly:

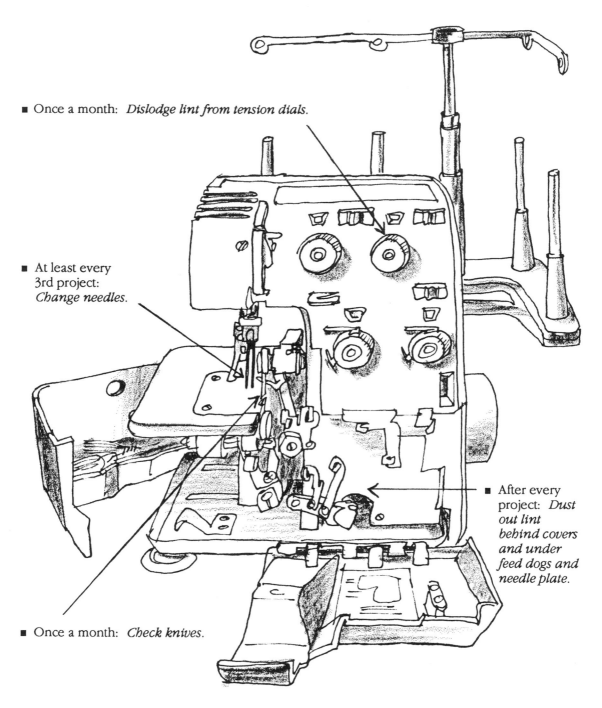

- Once a month: *Dislodge lint from tension dials.*

- At least every 3rd project: *Change needles.*

- After every project: *Dust out lint behind covers and under feed dogs and needle plate.*

- Once a month: *Check knives.*

Fig. 1-13: *Follow these basic guidelines to keep your serger running smoothly.*
- Once a year: *Take your serger to your local dealer for a checkup.*
- Every 12 - 15 serging hours: *Oil **only** if your model requires it.*

After every project

_____ Remove the presser foot, needle plate, and needle(s).

_____ Remove **large pieces of lint** with a fluffed-out lint brush.

_____ Blow out **fine lint** with environmentally-safe pressurized air, a hair dryer, a computer vacuum, or a household vacuum on reversed air flow. OR ...

_____ Use a lint brush lightly dipped in sewing machine oil to remove **fine lint** particles. The oil also provides some gentle lubrication.

 Note: Never blow into your serger to remove lint particles. The small amount of moisture in your breath can harm your machine.

At least every third project

_____ Change the needles.

■ Use the correct type and size of needle for your fabric.

■ Push the needle(s) all the way up into the needle bar.

■ Be sure the long groove is still toward the front after tightening the needle-retaining screw.

Every 12 to 15 hours of serging

 Note: Oil your serger, if it requires oiling at all (many models do not; see your manual). Use only sewing machine oil.

_____ If your serger is noisier than usual, oil it.

_____ If you haven't used your serger for several months, oil it before using it again.

_____ After oiling, test-serge on scraps of fabric to remove any residual oil.

Once a month

_____ Remove lint lodged in the tension discs.

■ Turn the tension dials to zero.

■ Put knotted thread through the tension discs.

■ Reset the tensions to normal and pull the knotted thread back and forth through the discs to remove any lint.

_____ Check the knives.

■ Do they cut ragged edges?

■ Do they have a shiny, worn look?

■ If so, replace the blade(s) (refer to your manual for instructions or see your local dealer).

Once a year

_____ Take your serger to your local dealer for an annual checkup.

_____ Stock up on needles, new accessories, and the latest books and information.

2. Ornamental Serging Basics

- Tension—The Key to Success
- Decorative Threads
- Threads Other Than Decorative
- Shaping Materials
- Other Important Serging Supplies
- Ornamental Serging Sample Book
- Exploring Your Machine's Creative Limits

Tension—The Key to Success

Once you have a thorough knowledge of serger tension adjustment, you will be able to use your machine to its fullest creative potential. On your sewing machine, you would change the tension only if there were something wrong with the stitch. *On a serger, you will need to readjust your tension settings practically every time you change your thread, fabric, or stitch type.* You'll also change tensions as you change the stitch length and width and when you want to create varied effects.

Although tension adjustment is part of any basic serger instruction, we will cover it again in this book because it is such a critical part of ornamental serging.

Changing serger tension settings is not complicated if you follow a few basic guidelines and know what a correctly adjusted stitch should look like. In a balanced 3-thread overlock stitch, the looper threads should hug the top and bottom of the fabric and overlock exactly on the edge. The needle thread should form a line along the left edge of the stitch and look like sewing machine straight-stitching on both top and bottom. (Fig. 2-1)

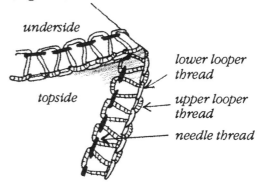

underside

topside

lower looper thread

upper looper thread

needle thread

Fig. 2-1: With balanced tension settings, the looper threads will hug the top and bottom of the fabric and overlock exactly on the edge.

See your manual or refer back to pages 12 - 14 for examples of perfectly balanced tension for all the stitch options on your *baby lock* model.

Practicing tension adjustment

If you have never experimented with your machine's tension settings, or if you have any doubt about how to adjust the serger tension properly, try this experiment:

1. Thread your serger with different colors of all-purpose or serger thread. (For easier identification, you may want to use the same colors as those on your thread guides.) If you have a 4-thread machine, remove the left needle and test first using a 3-thread overlock stitch. Later you can convert back to 4-thread and test that as well. Adjust for a medium-length (2.5mm to 3mm), balanced stitch.

2. Find the center of all your dial settings. If your dials turn from zero to nine, the center is five. If your machine has no dial numbers and the dial can be turned more than one full rotation, set the dials as close to the middle setting as possible. If you tend to forget which dial controls which looper or needle, write the names on a small piece of masking tape. Study your manual and place each label on the correct dial until you know them by heart.

3. Set the lower looper tension dial all the way to the left. At this point, the lower looper is at the loosest tension. Leave the upper looper and needle tension on the center setting.

4. Cut two 4" by 6" rectangles from medium-weight woven fabric. Serge-seam the rectangles together along one side and examine the results. Learn what the lower looper thread looks like when the tension is at its lowest (loosest) setting. Save your seam sample for your sample book (see page 33).

5. Next, set the dial of the lower looper tension almost all the way to the right, to the highest (tightest) setting. Leave the upper looper and needle tensions at the center setting. Repeat step 4, checking the results of a tightened lower looper tension. Save your sample.

6. Turn the lower looper tension back to the center and loosen the upper looper tension all the way to the left. Leave the lower looper and needle tension on the center setting. Repeat step 4, checking the results of a loosened upper looper tension. Save your sample.

7. Repeat step 5 for the upper looper by tightening the tension and leaving the lower looper and needle tensions on the center setting.

Balancing the tension

Now you are beginning to understand the effects of changing the tension settings on your serger—and you're no longer afraid to experiment! The next step is to learn how to adjust for a balanced tension:

1. Set the tension dials on their center settings.

2. Cut long 4"-wide strips from medium-weight woven fabric for testing. Put the right sides of two long strips together and serge a test seam for a few inches on the long edge.

3. Stop and look at the stitching behind the presser foot without removing the fabric. Examine the needle-thread line. If it is too loose, the seamline will pull open. If it is too tight, the seamline will pucker. (Fig. 2-2) Don't worry about the

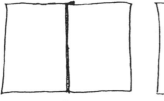

| too loose | too tight |

Fig. 2-2: When the needle tension is too loose, the seamline will pull open. When the needle tension is too tight, the seamline will pucker.

looper threads now. The needle-thread tension won't always need to be adjusted. Change the needle tension dial only if the seamline pulls open or looks puckered. Turn the dial to the right to tighten the tension or to the left to loosen it. Continue to test-serge and adjust—a few inches at a time—until the needle tension is balanced.

4. Now look at the upper and lower looper threads on your stitched sample. Remember, the looper threads should meet at the edge. If one thread is pulled *over* the edge, the other thread is too tight. First, find the one that appears to be too tight and **loosen** it. (Fig. 2-3) Serge a few more

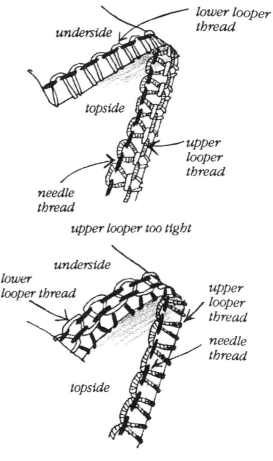

Fig. 2-3: Find looper tension that is too tight and loosen it.

inches. If the tension hasn't been improved, return the dial to the original position and **tighten** the other looper thread (the one that appears to be too loose).

Follow these guidelines to get perfectly balanced tension every time:

1. Adjust one dial at a time and test-serge after each adjustment. Don't make the mistake of turning all the tension dials at the same time.

2. Make only small adjustments. A small adjustment can make a big difference.

3. When adjusting the looper tension, first loosen the tension dial for the looper thread that appears to be too tight. If the adjustment doesn't seem to help the problem, or if it made it worse, **put that dial back where it was** and tighten the other looper tension dial. Continue adjusting, one dial at a time (putting the setting back where you started if the change did not help), until the tension is balanced.

4. Every time you use a different type of thread or fabric, you'll need to check your tension adjustments. For the most accurate adjustments, test-serge on scraps of the actual project fabric, using the same grain and the same number of layers.

5. Several serging and sewing pros use the jingle "righty-tighty, lefty-loosey" to teach the direction to turn a tension dial in order to tighten or loosen it. You might find it helpful, too, and it also applies to your sewing

machine tension dial and almost every screw.

Continue to practice, test, and experiment with varying fabrics and tensions. Learn to recognize what happens when you make tension adjustments. As you proceed through this book, you will find that *some very interesting novelty stitches can be formed by varying the tensions.* Both the rolled-edge stitch and flatlocking are created with tension adjustments. And that's only the beginning of a wide range of possibilities.

Confidence in using your serger and the ability to use it to its full potential come only after you are comfortable about changing your tensions.

Decorative Threads

We're constantly learning about new or newly discovered threads, yarns, ribbons, and trims that can be serged ornamentally. Creative serger enthusiasts have used everything from elastic thread to fine wire to create special ornamental effects.

Many materials for decorative serging can be found in the notions and trim departments of your local fabric store. Also try sewing machine dealerships; needlecraft, yarn, and craft shops; and mail-order sources.

Follow these selection guidelines as a starting point to test your ornamental serging possibilities:

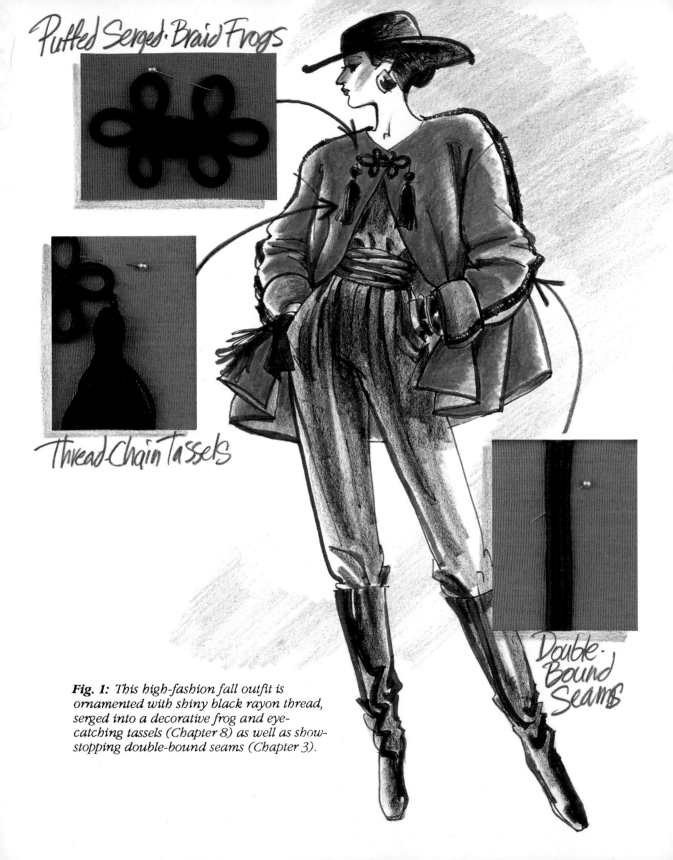

Puffed Serged-Braid Frogs

Thread-Chain Tassels

Double-Bound Seams

Fig. 1: *This high-fashion fall outfit is ornamented with shiny black rayon thread, serged into a decorative frog and eye-catching tassels (Chapter 8) as well as show-stopping double-bound seams (Chapter 3).*

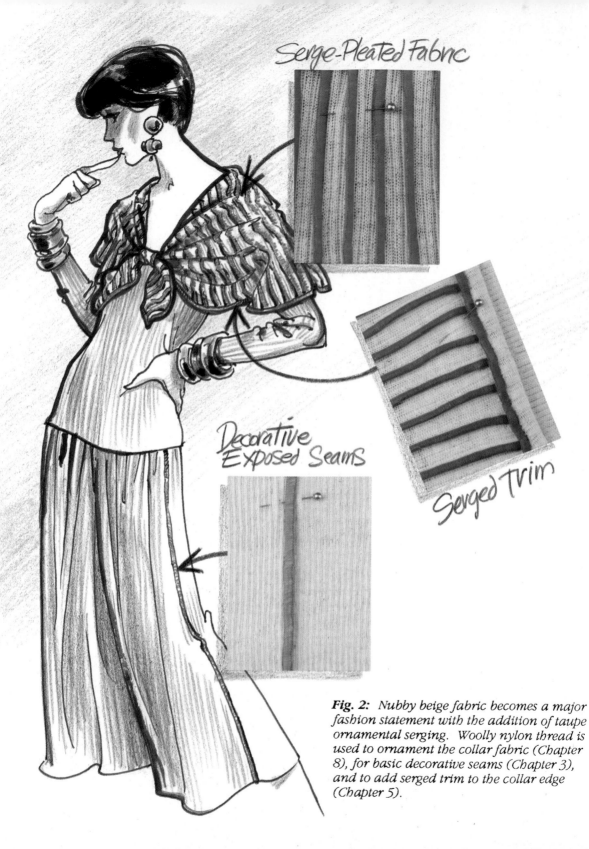

Serge-Pleated Fabric

Decorative Exposed Seams

Serged Trim

Fig. 2: *Nubby beige fabric becomes a major fashion statement with the addition of taupe ornamental serging. Woolly nylon thread is used to ornament the collar fabric (Chapter 8), for basic decorative seams (Chapter 3), and to add serged trim to the collar edge (Chapter 5).*

Fig. 3: Casual sportswear need not be plain. Black fringe emphasizes a yoke (Chapter 8) and coordinating serged-fold self braid (Chapter 5) adorns the neckline. A lapped and top-stitched zipper (Chapter 7) with matching fringe turns the utilitarian bag into a special creation.

Serged-Fold Self-Braid

Thread-Chain Fringe

Lapped & Top-stitched Zipper

Serger Cutwork

Double Rolled Edge

Serged Appliqué

Fig. 4: *Crisp and fresh, this pretty dress shows off three unusual serging techniques. The bib collar is bordered with a double rolled edge (Chapter 4) and accented with serger cutwork (Chapter 8). The handbag is ornamented with coordinating serger appliqué (also Chapter 8).*

Flat-locked Fringe

Fig. 5: *A businesslike suit is spiced up easily by adding serged piping (Chapter 5), serge-bound buttonholes (Chapter 7), and a focal-point tie with flatlocked-fringe edges (Chapter 6).*

Serged Piping

Serge-Bound Buttonholes

Elasticized Trim

Corded Flatlocking

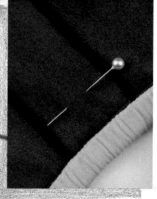

Elasticized Binding

Fig. 6: *This solid-color swimsuit sports ornamental serging to make it anything but ordinary. Corded flatlocking (Chapter 6) highlights the trunk portion. Contrasting elasticized binding keeps the legs securely in place and elasticized trim repeats the black accent color at the neckline (both Chapter 5).*

Serged Cording

Serged Couching

Thread-Chain Cording & Tassels

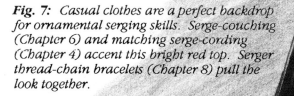

Fig. 7: *Casual clothes are a perfect backdrop for ornamental serging skills. Serge-couching (Chapter 6) and matching serge-cording (Chapter 4) accent this bright red top. Serger thread-chain bracelets (Chapter 8) pull the look together.*

**Balanced
Decorative
Edges**

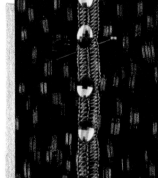

**Serged
Button Loops**

Fig. 8: *Even elegant evening wear can be enhanced with special serger techniques. Serged elastic button loops (Chapter 7), a balanced decorative edge (Chapter 4), and fluffy fishline ruffles (Chapter 6) are all featured in a coordinating metallic thread.*

Fishline Ruffles

Decorative Serging Quick Reference Chart

USE: N - Needle
UL - Upper Looper
LL - Lower Looper
SO - Serge Over
A - All Uses

EASE:
* Easy
** Moderate
*** Challenging

TENSION ADJUSTMENT: N - None
S - Slight
L - Lots

TYPE	SIZES AND COLORS AVAILABLE	USE	EASE OF USE	TENSION ADJUST-MENT	SUB-STITUTE	DESCRIPTION	APPLICATION	NOTES
Buttonhole Twist	Variety of colors.	A	*	N-S		Slightly heavier than all-purpose thread.	Edging or flatlock seaming all type sportswear, home decorator items.	May work satisfactorily in size 14 needle, not in size 11.
Woolly Nylon	Variety, including variegated.	A	*	S		Crimped, yarn-like thread, stretchy, fluffs up when serged. May melt with hot iron.	Excellent for providing soft elastic seams on lingerie, swimwear, activewear, silky, rolled edge.	May be used through needle. Tensions may need to be adjusted. Best coverage of any lightweight decorative thread.
Rayon	Variety of colors and sizes, including new "pearl" rayon.	A	*	N-S-L (depending on size)		Shiny, silk-like thread, smooth, bright colors.	High-luster edging or flatlock seaming for elegant fashion garments and accessories.	
Silk	Variety of colors and sizes.	A	*	N-S	Rayon Threads Machine Embroidery	Shiny, soft, smooth, expensive.	High-luster edging or flatlock seaming for elegant fashion garments and accessories.	
Metallics	Variety of sizes and colors, including variegated.	A	**	S-L		Adds glitter, can be used multi-strand or combined with other threads.	Highly decorative edge for sportswear, eveningwear, holiday gifts, and home decor.	Vary greatly according to manufacturer. Avoid those with coarse, metal fibers. Experiment to find which works best.
Braids	Variety of sizes, colors and fibers.	UL, LL, SO	** to ***	L		Purchase by the yard.	Edging or flatlock, seaming of garments, accessories, home decorator, and nusery items.	Require testing and experimentation to achieve tension balance. It may be necessary to bypass tension disc altogether. Use in loopers only.

Type	Description	Setting	Rating		Alternate	Characteristics	Uses	Tips
Ribbon	Variety of colors, fibers, including silk, acrylic, polyester 1/16 – 1/4" wide.	UL, LL, SO	***	L	Braided Rayon Ribbon	Soft knitting ribbon, bright colors.	Edging or flatlock, seaming of garments, accessories, home decorator, and nusery items.	Require testing and experimentation to achieve tension balance. It may be necessary to bypass tension disc altogether. Use in loopers only.
Braided Rayon Ribbon (Ribbon Floss)	Variety of colors, including metallic. 1/8" wide.	UL, LL, SO	**	L		Soft, knitting ribbon, bright color, crosswound on tube.	Edging or flatlock, seaming of garments, accessories, home decorator, and nusery items.	Require testing and experimentation to achieve tension balance. It may be necessary to bypass tension disc altogether. Use in loopers only.
Crochet Thread	Variety of colors, including variegated and metallic.	UL, LL, SO	** to ***	L		Available in acrylic and cotton, strong thread.	Edging or flatlock, seaming of garments, accessories, home decorator, and nusery items.	Require testing and experimentation to achieve tension balance. It may be necessary to bypass tension disc altogether. Use in loopers only.
Pearl Cotton	Variety of colors and sizes—#5 and 8 are most common.	UL, LL, SO	#8 ** #5***	L	Crochet thread Rayon "pearl"	Soft, shiny, tightly twisted strong thread.	Edging or flatlock, seaming of garments, accessories, home decorator, and nusery items.	Require testing and experimentation to achieve tension balance. It may be necessary to bypass tension disc altogether. Use in loopers only.
Yarns	Variety of colors Two- or three-ply, Baby or Sport yarn.	UL, LL, SO	*** (Two-ply easiest)	L	Pearl cotton Woolly stretch nylon	Soft, smooth, tightly twisted.	Edging or flatlock, seaming of garments, accessories, home decorator, and nusery items.	Require testing and experimentation to achieve tension balance. It may be necessary to bypass tension disc altogether. Use in loopers only.
Monofilament Nylon	Very fine Clear or smoke color. Variety of weights— #60 and #80 (finer) are common.	N, UL, LL (Use finer weights for needle.)	*	N		Strong, invisible thread, used with decorative thread, may melt with hot iron. The higher the number, the finer the thread.	Fashion accessories, home decorator items requiring strong seams, thread invisibility.	Some brands are too heavy and wiry to loop well. Look for lightweight, supple selection.
Elastic	Various sizes, including 1/4 – 3/8" widths.	A SO-1/4" & 3/8" widths	*	S		Adds stability and can create fabric.		
Machine Embroidery Lingerie	Variety of colors.	N, UL	**	N-S		Lightweight, smooth, delicate.	Lingerie, lightweight fabrics where stress is not a factor, edging soft fabrics.	

Special Tip: Decorative threads crosswound on top-feeding cones are easiest to use. (Fig. 2-4) Those wound in balls or skeins or sold by the yard are more difficult because they require extra care when serging in order to help them feed evenly.

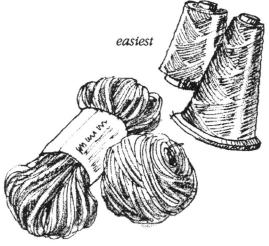

easiest

most difficult

Fig. 2-4: *Crosswound decorative thread is easiest to use. Balls and skeins are more difficult.*

Not all decorative threads will serge successfully in every machine. It's important always to test first. **Allow at least seven yards for each looper you'll be testing and two yards for each needle.** When estimating actual project yardage required, you'll need 10 times the finished decorative serging length for each looper.

Serging decorative threads

You have three options in serging decorative threads: threading through the loopers, threading through the needle, or serging over the ornamental thread.

Most often the decorative thread is threaded through the upper looper. This part of the stitch shows on the top side as you are serging. In a rolled edge (page 58) or reversible-edge binding (page 69), the upper looper should be the only thread visible on both sides.

If you want a balanced stitch (identical on both top and bottom), you'll also need to thread the lower looper with decorative thread. In some cases, when the thread is not strong, the lower looper will not be able to handle a thread that works in the upper looper. This is because the upper looper has fewer thread guides, which makes it easier to thread and puts less stress on the decorative thread.

The loopers don't pass through the fabric, so they both have larger eyes than a serger needle. This makes it possible to use thicker thread or yarn in your loopers. Consider these questions in determining whether a thread or yarn will work in the serger loopers:

1. When folded over double-layer, will the decorative thread easily pass through the looper eye? (Fig. 2-5)

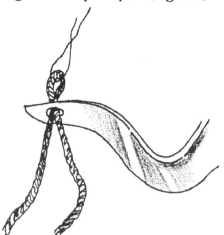

Fig. 2-5: Be sure your decorative thread or yarn will easily pass through the looper eye when it is doubled.

2. Is the thread flexible enough to form a uniform stitch without catching in the loopers?

3. Is the thread smooth or tightly twisted enough to ensure trouble-free feeding and prevent fraying or snagging?

4. Is the thread yardage continuous and long enough to complete the project? (Always allow extra yardage for testing; see page 25.)

Some lightweight threads also fit through the needle eye. Woolly nylon, fine metallic thread, lightweight monofilament nylon, and top-stitching thread are examples. These threads therefore can be used for the ladder side of flatlocking (see page 48) or for

other stitches that require loosened needle tension. In many cases, though, you will not need decorative thread in the needle, so use all-purpose or serger thread.

If a yarn, ribbon, or trim is too heavy or wide to fit through a looper or needle, you have the option of serging over it. To do this, the stitch must be wide enough to cover the trim without stitching into it. You also have the option of using a balanced, rolled-edge, or flatlock stitch, so test first for the best results.

When serging over any trim, insert it under the back of the presser foot and over the front. Make sure the trim is to the right of the needle and to the left of the knife. If your foot has an elastic/tape guide, thread the trim through the slots in the toe and the foot. (Fig. 2-6) Before inserting the

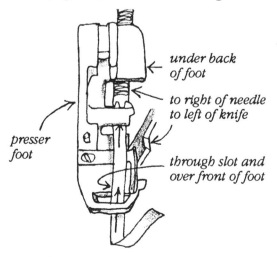

under back of foot

to right of needle to left of knife

presser foot

through slot and over front of foot

Fig. 2-6: Serge over trim for 1" to 2" before inserting fabric. Insert the trim through the elastic/tape guide if your foot has one.

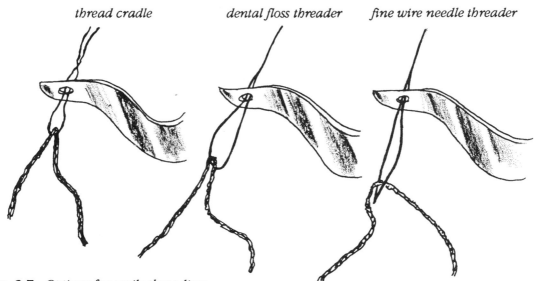

thread cradle *dental floss threader* *fine wire needle threader*

Fig. 2-7: *Options for easily threading heavy or limp decorative threads through looper eyes.*

fabric, turn the handwheel to form 1" to 2" of stitches over the trim. Always serge slowly. To highlight the trim rather than the stitching, use monofilament nylon or matching lightweight serger thread in the upper looper.

If the trim is bulky, remove the presser foot and guide the trim manually between the needle and the knife. Hold both the trim and the fabric taut. As we discuss corded edgings and other techniques requiring serging over threads or strands, we'll give more specific instructions for successful results.

Special threading tips

To begin, clip the thread you are using above the spool and tie on the decorative thread. Bypass the tension dial to prevent the knot from breaking or untying as it is pulled through. Pull the knot through the remaining thread guides. You may have to clip the knot at the eye of the looper or needle and thread it through manually.

Heavier or limp decorative threads are difficult to thread through the looper eyes. Serger pros use several tricks to do the job easily. Naomi makes a thread cradle by looping a strand of all-purpose thread around the specialty thread and then threads the ends of the all-purpose thread through the eye. (Fig. 2-7) Tammy uses a dental-floss threader (available at any drugstore) for the same purpose. Fine wire needle threaders are also available from sewing retailers and mail-order sources to simplify the threading process.

Rethread the tension dial and start serging with wide, long stitches. Gradually test and alter the stitch for the desired effect. For the most accurate results, always test scraps of the actual project fabric.

Turn the handwheel a few stitches to make sure the stitches are forming correctly. Then serge slowly for a few inches before stopping to adjust the tension. One general rule to keep in mind: the more resistance a thread has, the less tension it needs to have exerted on it. For example, a rough metallic thread needs less (looser) tension and a smooth, shiny rayon needs more tension.

If the tension is too tight after adjusting it all the way, remove the thread from the tension dial. If it is too loose, try wrapping the thread around the tension dial twice. (Fig. 2-8)

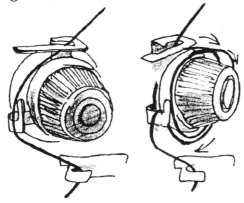

for less tension   for more tension

Fig. 2-8: *When the tension dial cannot be adjusted further, remove the thread for less tension or wrap it a second time for more tension.*

 Special Tip: Tensions and stitch length can vary from machine to machine, even on the same model. Your dealer cannot expand the range but can adjust the ranges slightly in one direction or the other.

Adjust to the desired stitch length. Most decorative seams and edges are serged with a satin (short) stitch length. There should be enough thread coverage so little, if any, fabric shows through the serging. If you adjust the serger for too short a stitch length, though, the fabric may jam under the presser foot or the seam may pucker. The thickness of the thread and the type of fabric you use will determine how short a stitch length you need. Finer thread requires a shorter stitch length for maximum coverage, while heavier thread looks good with a slightly longer stitch length. (Fig. 2-9)

finer thread—   heavier thread—
shorter stitch   longer stitch

Fig. 2-9: *For maximum coverage, use a shorter stitch length for finer thread. Lengthen slightly for heavier thread.*

When shortening the stitch length, you will also need to tighten both looper tensions or the stitching will hang off the edge of the fabric. (Fig. 2-10)

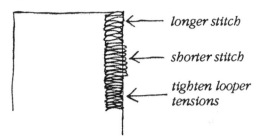

longer stitch

shorter stitch

tighten looper tensions

Fig. 2-10: *Tighten both looper tensions when shortening stitch so stitches won't hang off edge.*

Because decorative stitching is an important part of the design of a garment or project, the stitches must be smooth and uniform. The slightest pulling of the decorative thread can narrow the stitch or even break the strand. (Fig. 2-11)

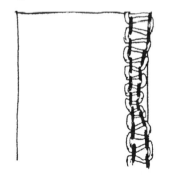

Fig. 2-11: *Stitches will narrow or break if the decorative thread does not feed evenly.*

If uneven stitches are a problem, check for anything that may be causing uneven feeding of your decorative thread. One common problem is that the thread catches on the spool itself or winds around the spool pin under the spool. Make sure the thread is feeding evenly off the spool.

You can also use spool caps or thread nets to control feeding of slippery or wiry thread. For threads wound on balls or skeins, rewind the thread loosely by hand onto empty cones or spools. Thread and yarn rewinding can be done quickly with a cone-winder, sold in knitting shops.

Some serger pros prefer simply reeling off several yards at a time from the ball or skein while serging. With this method, be sure that the feeding is not impeded by sewing tools cluttering your work area.

To illustrate how important even feeding can be, our serging friend Sue Green tells an amusing story. As she was working with decorative yarn in her upper looper, she kept getting uneven stitches (which she calls hiccups) in her serging. After checking all the usual trouble spots, she discovered that her kitten was playing with the ball of yarn on the floor. Even though she was pulling off the yarn as she serged, the kitten's extra pulling occasionally caused just enough tension change to create major glitches in her otherwise perfect decorative stitching.

Combining thread types

You may need to make additional tension adjustments when you are combining different thread types and using them in the same looper simultaneously. We do this for special decorative effects, such as adding a shiny fine metallic thread to woolly nylon or for toning down the color blocking of a variegated thread using one solid color thread or another strand of the same thread with the colors aligned differently. Another thread commonly combined with a decorative one is fine elastic thread, because it adds stretch-prevention to serged edges and seams.

When combining thread types, make sure both are feeding evenly without restrictions. You may need to adjust the tension or remove one of the threads from a tension dial. Always test first before serging your actual project.

Pressing over decorative thread

Some types of decorative thread (such as woolly nylon, monofilament nylon, and pearl cotton) are sensitive to a hot iron. For best results, use a press cloth to prevent melting or a permanent shine on your thread. (Fig. 2-12) Consider the fiber content of the thread and treat it similarly to a fabric of the same type. If in doubt, test first.

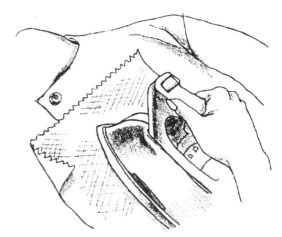

Fig. 2-12: *Use a press cloth to prevent melting or shine on sensitive decorative thread.*

Threads Other Than Decorative

All-purpose or serger thread: All-purpose thread is most often cotton-covered polyester, wound parallel on conventional spools. Serger thread usually has the same fiber content but is a little lighter in weight than all-purpose thread. It is crosswound on cones or tubes so that it will feed more evenly, in an upward direction, during higher-speed serger sewing.

Monofilament nylon thread: Used for many serger techniques, this handy thread comes in either clear or smoke shades. We prefer the lighter-weight size 80 thread for use in either the needle or loopers. Monofilament nylon is practically invisible for covering serger-applied trims and for "floating" stitches on top of the fabric. Because the nylon also is strong, you can use it in the lower looper for tightening down a rolled edge or for perfecting other techniques. Be careful to prevent melting when pressing this thread.

Fusible thread: A special thread combined with a heat-activated component, this exciting new product bonds easily at the touch of a steam iron (much like fusible interfacing). Fusible thread helps stabilize and position edges and seam allowances in a wide variety of decorative techniques. We also use it to position serged braid or cord for couching and monogramming. Always test your application first on your project fabric.

Although top-stitching may be added for extra security, the pliable fusible thread bond withstands both washing and dry cleaning. For maximum fusing coverage, we usually use it in the lower looper of a 3- or 4-thread serged stitch or in the needle of a 2-thread overedge stitch. The more fusible thread exposed, the better the bond. When you use this thread in the lower looper, tighten the tension slightly so the thread does not extend past the edge of the fabric.

Always press from the top side of the stitching. Never allow the iron to touch the fusible thread directly. Because the fusible component has a low melting point, press-baste first with a warm iron. Then permanently bond using as much steam and heat as your fabric will tolerate. Allow the bond to cool before moving the fabric. Also, quickly secure seam ends with a shot of steam applied over (but not touching) the thread chain.

Shaping Materials

Clear elastic: About one-third the thickness of regular elastic, clear polyurethane elastic does not "grow" as it is stitched through. It is also impervious to nicks from serger knives. Handy for many sewing and serging projects, it comes in five widths—1/8", 1/4", 3/8", 1/2", and 3/4".

Elastic thread: Available in a range of colors and sizes (from lightweight to cording), elastic thread has several interesting serger applications. All but the heaviest weights can be threaded through the loopers (see Lesson 34, Serged Elastic Button Loops, page 146). Elastic thread can also be serged over to create shirring or to stabilize an edge.

Fishline: If you don't already have some on hand, fishline is available at most sporting goods, discount, and drug stores. We use it for decoratively ruffling edges. Choose the clear line to avoid show-through in your project. Fishline weights vary from 12 lb. to 40 lb. Use the 12 lb. for lightweight fabrics and a heavier weight for heavier fabrics, serging over two layers, or for extra body.

Fine wire: Wire, used to shape ornamental edges, is available in any craft store. Fine, lightweight floral wire is usually precut to 18" lengths. For projects that require longer lengths, try beading wire, which comes on spools and in a variety of colors and weights.

Batting: Various weights of batting are available in both cotton and polyester. We prefer either bonded batting, which holds together well, or fleece, which is a little thinner.

Fiberfill: This shredded batting is most often polyester and is used to stuff pillows and craft projects.

Other Important Serging Supplies

- Your *baby lock* serger

- Your owner's manual and all machine attachments and accessories (including tweezers and screwdrivers)

- A straight-stitch sewing machine, preferably with zigzag capability

- Needle-nosed pliers or needle inserter

- Extra serger needles

- Extra serger knife blade (one comes with your serger)

- Wire threader or dental-floss threader

- Thread nets (some are included with your machine)

- Spool caps

- Seam sealant like *Fray Check*

- Washable glue stick

- Fusible transfer web (such as *Wonder-Under*)

- Stabilizers—both tear-away and water-soluble

- Dressmaker shears

- Rotary cutter and mat

- Seam ripper

- Yardstick

- Tape measure

- Washable and air-erasable marking pens

- Machine lint brush or canned air

- Loop turner, darning needle, or crochet hook

- Any other favorite sewing supplies

Fig. 2-13: *Keep a sample book of notes, test results, and creative ideas.*

Ornamental Serging Sample Book

We recommend that you keep a sample book of all your lesson results and other testing for later reference. One perfect way to do this is to use a *baby lock* "Owner's Workbook" (available for many models) and add extra pages for additional samples. (Fig. 2-13) Or use a standard 3-ring binder with heavy paper to mount your finished samples.

Be sure to note your tension, stitch width, and stitch-length settings for each type of stitch, thread, and fabric used. This information will be handy as a starting point for your future projects.

Put creative ideas in your sample book, too. Clip magazine photos, write notes about techniques to try, and add special instructions that come with new types of thread or other ornamental serging supplies. Refer to your sample book for inspiration and information while planning and completing each new serger project.

Exploring Your Machine's Creative Limits

As you work through this book, you'll no doubt come up with bright ideas of your own. Because serger sewing is a relatively new art, there are lots of techniques and ideas yet to be discovered and developed.

Be open to experimentation. Test new serger techniques. Read in our newsletter and other publications about the latest techniques. Think about how you can adapt them for your own use. Then take time to answer the following questions in order to inspire your creative efforts:

1. *How can I adapt new sewing products and threads for serger use?* With so many recent technical advances, new serging possibilities abound. Fusible thread (page 31) opened up a wealth of new techniques for us. Clear elastic and elastic thread (page 31) add even more options. Interesting new decorative threads (pages 23 and 24) continue to be introduced.

2. *How can I combine craft products and ideas with my serging skills?* Many of our latest techniques and projects have come from using craft items such as fine wire (Lesson 8), water-soluble stabilizer (Lesson 37), and beads (Lesson 28).

3. *Can I convert sewing techniques for the serger in order to speed up a project or make it more durable?* Fishline ruffles (Lesson 8), lettuced edges (Lesson 5), and French seams (Lesson 1) are a breeze with the help of a serger.

4. *Are there unique stitch configurations on the serger that I can use for unusual ornamental effects?* Serger lace (Lesson 24), reversible-edge binding (Lesson 9), and serger chain art (Lesson 35) were all developed because of the machine's unique stitching capabilities.

5. *Is there another way to manipulate an edge or a fold to get a different result?* Double-bound seams (Lesson 2) and edges (Lesson 14), and double rolled edges (Lessons 5 and 19) are some recent options.

6. *Can I copy a trim or decorative effect from ready-to-wear?* Look in stores, magazines, and catalogs for inspiration. Check out craft projects, too.

The more you use your serger and experiment with all its ornamental options, the easier you'll find it is to be creative and to develop ideas of your own. So start now to explore all the possibilities and really use your *baby lock* to its creative limits.

3. Decorative Seams

- ■ **Lesson 1. Basic Seams**
- ■ **Lesson 2. Serge-bound Seams**
- ■ **Lesson 3. Flatlocked Seams**

Serging seams is one of the most basic uses for your serger. The type of fabric, the amount of stress placed on the seam during wearing, and personal preference are all factors in deciding which seam to use.

Any seam may be hidden on the inside or used ornamentally, exposed on the right side of the fabric. Exposed seams are especially popular on many of today's sportier ready-to-wear garments.

When seams are exposed, they become a decorative design element. Therefore, it is important that the tension and stitches are perfect, no matter what kind of thread you use. Always test first with two layers of the project fabric and the same thread you will be using. Compare your samples with the illustrations of perfect stitch formation in your manual or on pages 12 - 14 and adjust accordingly.

When serging decorative seams, the method you use to secure seam ends is important. When a seam will be crossed by another serged seam, we usually don't secure the ends by any other method. The serged thread chains hold the ends in place until

they can be seamed across and secured. If additional reinforcement is needed, we straight-stitch along the needleline of the second seam for about 2" to 3" across the first seam. (Fig. 3-1)

Fig. 3-1: *Serged seams are often secured by another seam. Straight stitching can add reinforcement.*

When the seam ends will not be crossed and secured with another serged seam, we must secure them with another method. The deciding factor is usually how much the method of securing will show. Because exposed seams are on the outside of the fabric and not worn next to the skin, our first choice is to use a drop of seam sealant on the ends. Be sure to let the sealant dry thoroughly before cutting the chain.

S **Special Tip:** If the wet seam sealant accidentally touches another part of the project, leaving a stain, rub the spot with a cotton swab soaked in rubbing alcohol. The stain will disappear.

Lesson 1. Basic Seams

When seaming, it is important to serge-trim some of the fabric, even if it is just enough to neaten the edges. This ensures even stitching, neater edges, and better control of the width trimmed. It is easiest to trim between 1/8" and 3/8".

A basic seam can be serged with either a 3- or 4-thread stitch. The 2-thread overedge stitch will form a *flatlocked* seam (see page 48), but will not form a basic *locking* seam. If the seam will not be top- or edge-stitched but you want the seam to be as secure as possible, use a 4-thread stitch or straight stitch along the needleline after serging a 3-thread seam.

Basic decorative seam

To serge a decorative, exposed seam, place the fabric wrong sides together and serge with the needle on the seamline. (When using two needles, the left needle will be on the seamline.) Both sides of the seam will show, so use the same type of thread in both the upper and lower loopers. You may decide to use the same color for both loopers or to vary the colors to achieve a desired effect. Depending on the seam placement, you may not need to press (see our Double-Bow Pillow project, page 40).

Exposed seams are often pressed to one side and top-stitched for neatness or to add strength. In this case, only the seam's upper looper thread will show. Apply top-stitching right next to the overlocked edge using a long stitch length. For more accuracy, use the blindhem foot on your sewing machine to guide your stitching evenly. Adjust the foot so the overlocked edge is next to the guide. (Fig. 3-2)

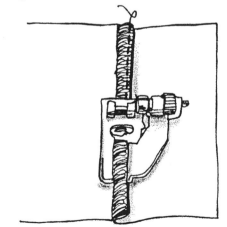

Fig. 3-2: *Use sewing machine blindhem foot to top-stitch decorative seam to one side.*

To secure an exposed seam quickly, put fusible thread (see page 31) in the lower looper when serging the seam. Before serging, determine to which side the seam will be pressed and position that side on the bottom. Tighten the lower looper tension slightly so the fusible thread does not show from the right side. Serge-seam. Carefully press-baste the seam to the side, then steam thoroughly to permanently fuse. For most seams, no other securing is needed.

Hidden lapped serging technique

We often need to lap decorative stitching—when completing a circle, joining the ends of an opening, or (occasionally) correcting irregular areas of serging. This technique eliminates the need to serge on and off the fabric, which provides a neater (almost invisible) decorative finish.

1. Raise the needle(s) and presser foot and disengage the stitch from the stitch finger.

2. Insert your fabric, positioning the needle(s) on the seamline. If you are joining ends of an opening or correcting irregular serging, position the needle(s) about 1/2" before the end of one side of the opening. (Fig. 3-3)

3. Serge until you reach the opposite end of the decorative stitching.

4. Disengage the knife (to prevent cutting the original stitching) and overlap the stitches for 1/2".

5. Raise the presser foot and needle(s), and pull the fabric just behind the needle(s). (Fig. 3-4)

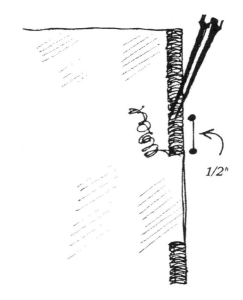

Fig. 3-3: *Position the needles 1/2" before the end of the opening.*

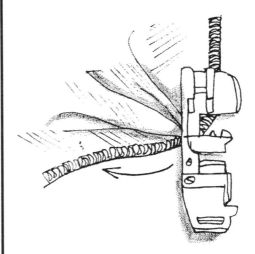

Fig. 3-4: *Raise the needles and presser foot, and pull the fabric behind the needle(s).*

6. Then serge off the fabric to form a chain of thread.

7. If you're using a heavy decorative thread, dab on a drop of seam sealant and trim the chain when dry. If you're using a satin stitch and a lighter-weight decorative thread (such as woolly stretch nylon), lapping the stitches should secure them adequately. Simply trim away the excess thread chain after lapping the stitches.

If you are lapping decorative serging and plan to trim the edge, trim away a 2" section of the seam allowance to the serger cutting line where you plan to begin your serging. (Fig. 3-5) Then position the cutting line against the blade before starting.

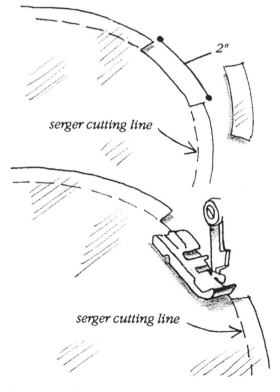

Fig. 3-5: When trimming the edge, cut away 2" to position the knife on the cutting line.

Basic seam for reversibles

Basic exposed seams can also be used for two-layer reversibles, leaving exposed decorative seams on one side and a seamline on the other. Sandwich the fabric of the seamline side (right sides together) inside the fabric of the exposed-seam side (right sides out). The wrong sides of the two fabrics will be together. Serge-seam. Open the layers and top-stitch the seam allowances to one side. (Fig. 3-6)

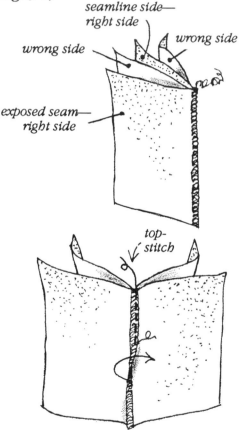

Fig. 3-6: Sandwich fabric layers for reversibles. One side will have a seamline. The other side will have an exposed and top-stitched decorative seam.

Lapped seam

A lapped seam is formed by serge-finishing the edges of both layers of fabric separately, then top-stitching one to the other. Serge-finish both layers with the needle on the seamline. Overlap the edges, matching the seamlines. Top-stitch on the needleline, then top-stitch along the opposite side of the seam if desired. (Fig. 3-7)

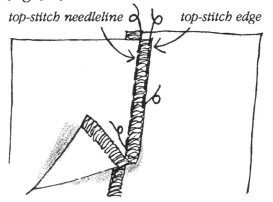

top-stitch needleline   top-stitch edge

Fig. 3-7: *For a lapped seam, serge-finish both edges. Top-stitch together along needleline. Top-stitch again on the edge if desired.*

Lapped seams are flat and very durable and are also used for reversibles. The upper looper thread on the top fabric layer is the only exposed part of the seam. For reversibles, both layers are serge-finished with one upper looper thread exposed on each side of the garment. Top-stitch on the matched needlelines only.

Decorative French seam

Serged French seams on the outside of a garment or project form a decorative detail resembling a tuck. With the fabric right sides together, serge a narrow, medium-length, 3-thread seam. Fold the wrong sides of the fabric over the seam and press carefully. Straight-stitch next to the cut edges, enclosing the seam. Use your sewing machine's blindhem foot to sew a perfectly even width, placing the fold of the seam next to the guide on the foot. This ornamental French seam works best on straight seams. (Fig. 3-8)

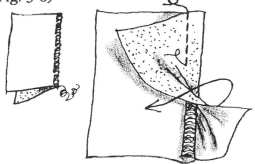

Fig. 3-8: *For exposed French seam, serge narrow seam with right sides together. Wrap fabric to enclose serging and straight stitch.*

Mock flat-felled seam

The mock flat-felled seam, simple yet durable, is used on heavy fabrics. Top-stitching with decorative thread adds ornamental interest to your finished project. Right sides together, straight-stitch the seam with a 5/8" seam allowance. Serge-finish the edges together and press them to one side. For extra strength, use fusible thread in the lower looper when serge-finishing and fuse the allowances to one side. From the right side, top-stitch over the allowances right next to the seamline and again 1/4" away. Use a decorative thread like buttonhole twist in the needle and a long stitch length.

Project: Double-Bow Pillow

˙Exposed satin-stitched seams become a decorative detail on this attention-getting pillow. It's simple to serge and requires only 3/4 yard of fabric. (Fig. 3-9)

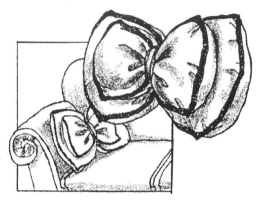

Fig. 3-9: *Double-bow pillow features decorative seams-out detail.*

Stitch: 4-thread overedge or
   3-thread
Stitch length: Short (1mm)
Stitch width: Medium to wide
Thread: Contrasting color to fabric
   Needle(s): All-purpose or serger
   Upper looper: Decorative
   Lower looper: Decorative
Tension: Balanced
Needle(s): Size 11/75
Fabric: 3/4 yard 45"-wide solid or
   print cotton chintz
Notions: Polyester fiberfill

1. Cut two 14" by 20" rectangles, two 12" by 16" rectangles, and one 6-1/2" by 12" rectangle.

2. Adjust your serger for a satin-length, 4-thread overedge stitch. To create an unusual textured border, tighten the right needle tension. Or, if desired, use a 3-thread satin stitch. (Fig. 3-10)

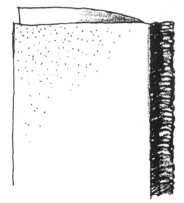

Fig. 3-10: *Satin-length 4-thread overedge stitch forms a pretty, textured seam.*

3. Raise the needle(s) and presser foot and clear the stitch finger. Place the two large rectangles wrong sides together. Insert the fabric under the presser foot, positioning the needle(s) on the seamline 2" past the center of one long side (see the hidden lapped serging technique, page 37). Serge-seam, barely trimming the four edges to neaten. Serge on and off at the four corners and end the stitching about 5" from the beginning serging. Lightly stuff the pillow with fiberfill and serge-seam the opening closed using the hidden lapped serging technique.

4. Repeat step 3 for the pair of smaller rectangles.

5. Fold the remaining rectangle in half lengthwise with the wrong sides together. Using a longer (3mm) stitch length, serge-seam the long edge. Refold with the seam in the center of the strip and serge-finish both ends.

6. Center the smaller pillow section over the larger one. With the seam underneath, wrap the serged strip from step 5 around the center of both pillows to form a tie. Hand-tack the strip on the back side of the pillow to secure.

Lesson 2.
Serge-bound Seams

One of the first things we learn about the serger is that it neatly finishes seams by overlocking the edges. Developing this feature further, we can vary stitch length, width, and thread used to decoratively serge-finish seam allowances. We can also use the serger to speedily encase seam allowances in binding fabric.

Decorative serge-bound seams can be so attractive that we often choose to feature them on the outside of a project. This works especially well for jackets and coats because the seam allowance is featured ornamentally on the outside, while the inside shows only a neat seamline.

A professional-looking binding must be a consistent width. With the serger's exacting cutting ability and the even width of serger stitches, a consistent-width serged binding is almost foolproof.

Serged seam binding

This decorative seam finish is usually seen on the inside of unlined coats or jackets. It is easily achieved by finishing the seam-allowance edges with decorative, satin-length serging and then sewing the seam with a 5/8" seam allowance. (Fig. 3-11)

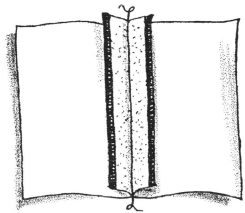

Fig. 3-11: For serged seam binding, finish allowance edges with satin-length serging before seaming.

Remove the left needle. Put a contrasting-color or tone-on-tone decorative thread in the upper looper. Adjust for a short (1 - 1.5mm) stitch length and a medium to narrow stitch width. Serge-finish from the right side of the fabric, barely skimming the four edge. We like to experiment with different stitch widths, depending upon the type of thread we use. Finer thread needs more coverage and looks best with a narrow stitch width. Heavier thread is often more attractive in a wider stitch. Also try woolly nylon or glossy pearl rayon thread for attractive serged seam bindings.

Serged French binding

For a couture effect, add serged French binding to seams, using a contrasting or matching strip of fabric. Try combining different types and colors of fabrics for stronger emphasis. Nylon *Lycra* works well as binding fabric because it folds tightly against the seam allowance. In addition, its bright colors can add a stunning contrast to dark or basic colored fabric. Try binding velvet with satin, wool with lightweight synthetic suede, or woven fabric with knits.

1. For a finished binding of approximately 1/4", cut a binding strip 1" wide (four times the desired finished width). The width of the finished binding should be no wider than the width of your serger's widest stitch. If the seams to be bound are straight, the strip can be cut on the crosswise grain. However, if the bound seams are even slightly curved, cut the strip on the bias for wovens or in the direction of greater stretch for knits (usually crossgrain).

2. Adjust for a 7.5mm stitch width (or the widest on your machine) and a medium stitch length. From the wrong side, with fusible thread in the lower looper, serge-finish one long binding edge, trimming a scant 1/8". We like to take advantage of the 7.5mm stitch width of either the 4-thread overedge stitch or the 4-thread

mock safety stitch for the widest possible serged French binding.

3. Because the binding strip has a 1/4" seam allowance, it may be easier for you also to pretrim the fabric seam allowances to 1/4". Or serge the seam and trim it before applying the binding. As you become more comfortable with the application, you'll be able to serge-seam with a full seam allowance and apply the binding simultaneously. (Fig. 3-12) This one-step method is

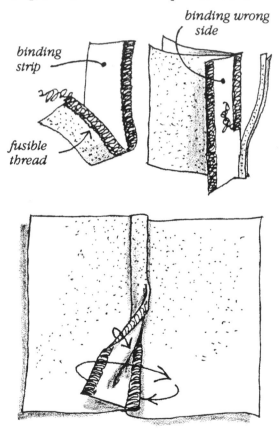

Fig. 3-12: For serged French binding, finish binding-strip edge with fusible thread in lower looper. Serge-seam binding and fabric together. Wrap binding around seam allowance and fuse in place.

the easiest and fastest unless the fabric is difficult to manage. If the fabric is rigid, slippery, or must be held taut while serging, straight-stitch or baste the seam first and trim the seam allowances to 1/4" before applying the binding.

Place the right sides of the fabric together, aligning the binding strip on top over the seamline, fusible side down. (To position serged French binding on the outside of your garment, place the fabric wrong sides together.) Serge-seam the unfinished edges, leaving a 1/4" seam allowance. The needleline of the serging should be on the seamline of the project. (If desired, you may change back to serger thread in the lower looper before serge-seaming.) Do not stretch while serging-seaming straight binding. For outer curves, ease the binding slightly, and for inner curves stretch it slightly. Wrap the binding around the seam allowance to encase it. Carefully press-baste to position the binding, then steam-press to fuse securely.

If you are applying a French binding without fusible thread, it is unnecessary to serge-finish one long edge of the binding. Serge-seam the binding to the fabric, wrap the binding around the seam allowance, press, and stitch-in-the-ditch. Trim the unfinished long edge of the binding close to the stitching on the underside. Press the

binding to one side and top-stitch next to the folded edge to secure. (Fig. 3-13)

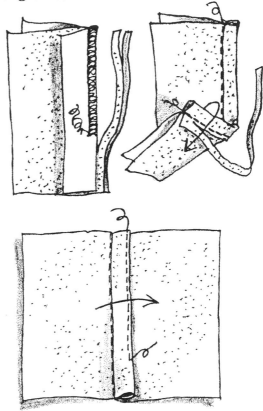

Fig. 3-13: *Without using fusible thread, make a French binding by serge-seaming the strip to the fabric. Wrap the strip around the seam allowance and stitch-in-the-ditch. Trim unfinished edge, then top-stitch binding to one side.*

Double-bound seam

A self-bound seam takes some extra time and skill to construct, but it is very durable and a real show-stopper. Both seam allowances are wrapped with self fabric, then decoratively serged from the right side. Using a 7.5mm stitch width, finished decorative seams can be as wide as 1/2". This double binding method will be adapted for edges and decorative detail in later lessons.

1. To allow the extra fabric needed for wrapping a 1/4" seam allowance, before cutting out your garment or project, add an additional 1/2" to each edge that will be bound.

2. With right sides together, straight-stitch a seam using the seam allowance recommended on your pattern. (The seam allowance is usually 5/8" but may be 1/2" on decorative home projects.)

3. Press the seam allowances open and trim one allowance to a scant 1/4". From the right side, wrap the fabric securely around the trimmed allowance, forming a 1/4" fold. Press. (Fig. 3-14)

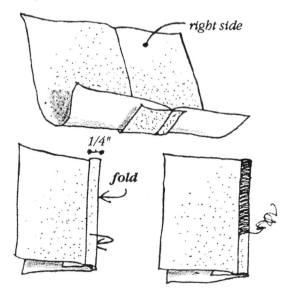

Fig. 3-14: Make a double-bound seam by trimming the right allowance and wrapping fabric around it. Serge-finish the fold.

Special Tip: To minimize bulk on fabrics that do not ravel easily, test-trim the seam allowance to 1/8" before wrapping, then still press the 1/4" fold.

4. Use decorative thread in the upper and lower loopers and serger thread in the needle(s). Adjust for a wide, short (1-2mm) stitch. We love the 7.5mm-wide stitch on several *baby lock* 4-thread overedge models for the widest possible binding. If your serger does not have the 7.5mm width, use the widest stitch. On 4-thread mock safety stitch machines, convert to your widest 3-thread stitch (remove the left needle) to provide complete coverage of the bound seam. For a stitch width narrower than 7.5mm, adjust the fold width so that the serged stitch will cover the entire fold. Test first.

5. With the knife disengaged to prevent cutting the fabric, serge along the fold from the right side of the fabric. The needle (the left needle on the 4-thread overedge stitch) should be on the seamline. Adjust the tension so the overlocked stitches are tight against the fold.

6. Repeat steps 3 to 5 for the other seam allowance. When serging, make sure the needle stitches are right on or just inside the needleline of the first row of serging. (You will be serging in the direction opposite the first row of serging.) (Fig. 3-15)

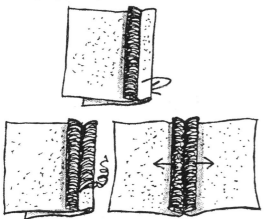

Fig. 3-15: *Trim, wrap, and serge the other allowance, overlapping needlelines. Press allowances open.*

7. Press the seam allowances open on the right side of the fabric. Use a press cloth, if necessary, to prevent melting the thread or leaving a shine.

Optional: If you will be securing the finished double-bound seam to the fabric, use decorative thread in the upper looper only. Use serger thread in the needle(s) and lower looper. Top-stitch along each side of the binding. Or you may choose to use fusible thread in the lower looper when serge-finishing the folds, so you can fuse the binding to the fabric.

Double-piped seam

For this variation of the double-bound seam, we follow the same procedure, but we use a narrow balanced stitch or the 4-thread mock safety stitch on the 1/4" folds. The seam allowance will need to be trimmed to 1/4" (not narrower) so that it will catch in the narrower decorative serging and not pull out.

Note that with this technique part of the fabric will show between the two sides of the binding. With a narrow balanced stitch, the needlelines will not overlap. (Fig. 3-16) With a

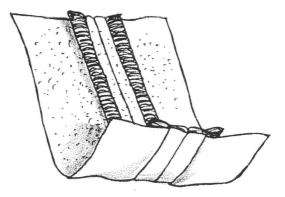

Fig. 3-16: *The double-piped seam is a double-bound seam serged with a narrow balanced stitch.*

4-thread mock safety stitch, the left needlelines will overlap on the seamline, but fabric will still be visible between the two needlelines on both allowances. Alter stitch characteristics to vary the effect.

Project: Hobo Bag

A double-bound seam is featured on this easy-to-make, versatile bag. Vary the pattern size for different uses or to suit your personal style. (Fig. 3-17)

Fig. 3-17: *Easy hobo bag features double-bound seam.*

Stitch: 4-thread overedge or 3-thread
Stitch length: Short (1 - 2mm)
Stitch width: Widest
Thread: Contrasting color
    Needles(s): All-purpose or serger
    Upper looper: Woolly nylon
    Lower looper: Woolly nylon, serger thread, or fusible thread

Tension: Balanced
Needle(s): Size 11/75
Fabric: 3/4 yard 45"-wide water repellent fabric or soft upholstery fabric
Notions: 1" D-rings—1 pair; 3/4"-wide *Velcro*—20"; 1"-wide cotton or nylon strap— 1 yard

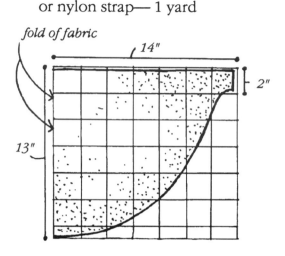

Fig. 3-18: *Hobo bag pattern grid—each square is 2".*

1. Cut two bag pieces using the pattern grid.

2. Center one piece of *Velcro* on each wrong side of the top of the bag. Adjust for a medium stitch length and width. From the right side, serge each top of the bag, catching the *Velcro* in the stitching.

 Special Tips: When serging with *Velcro*, do not use woolly nylon in the looper that carries stitches onto the *Velcro* piece. The woolly nylon's crimped fibers can catch on the *Velcro*'s hooks and loops. Also test the stitch length first. You may have to lengthen the stitch when serging over *Velcro*.

3. Top-stitch the lower edge of the *Velcro* to each side of the bag.

4. With the right sides of the bag pieces together, straight stitch around the lower edge with a 1/4" seam allowance. Wrap the fabric around one seam allowance and press lightly (see Fig. 3-14).

5. Serge along the fold with the knife disengaged.

6. Repeat steps 4 and 5 for the other seam allowance.

7. Press open the seam allowances on the outside of the bag. Then top-stitch the bound seam allowances to the bag.

Optional: To secure the seam allowances to the bag, use fusible thread in the lower looper when serge-finishing the fold.

8. Serge across both narrow ends with fusible thread in the lower looper. Wrap each end around a D-ring. Fuse and top-stitch to secure the D-ring. (Fig. 3-19)

Fig. 3-19: Secure D-rings and straps by serge-finishing with fusible thread. Fuse into position and top-stitch to reinforce.

9. Serge-finish each end of the strap with fusible thread in the lower looper. Insert each end of the strap through a D-ring. Fuse and top-stitch to secure.

Lesson 3. Flatlocked Seams

A flatlocked seam is always exposed on both sides of the fabric, so it can be used to add an interesting design detail. We most often see flatlocked seams on delicate lingerie and other garments on which sturdy seams are not essential. Although a flatlocked seam is relatively secure, it is not your most durable option.

Perfecting flatlocking

The 2-thread overedge and 3-thread overlock stitches are most commonly used for flatlocking. A 2-thread flatlock uses less thread and therefore makes a finer, lighter-weight, and flatter seam. For both 2-thread and 3-thread flatlocking, the needle thread is loosened so that it overlocks with the looper thread past the edge of the fabric. Because the needle thread is so loose, the seam can be pulled open until it lies flat. (Fig. 3-20)

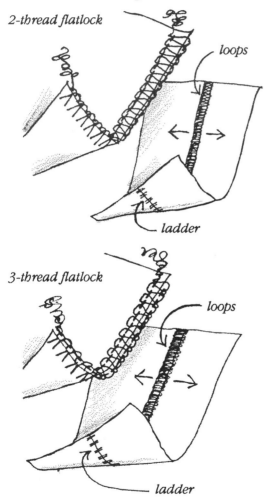

2-thread flatlock

loops

ladder

3-thread flatlock

loops

ladder

Fig. 3-20: *To flatlock, loosen needle thread. Allow stitches to hang off edge. Pull flat after serging.*

The perfect flatlocked seam should be pulled completely flat. To do this, you must allow the stitches to hang off the edge as you serge. Feed the fabric under the presser foot slightly away from the knife. Your stitches will interlock beyond the edge, and you'll never have to worry about the knife cutting your fabric. No amount of pressing will correct a flatlocked seam that cannot be pulled completely flat. Use a blindhem foot (or ornamental stitching guide) to guide the edge evenly.

When flatlock seaming, you must trim the edges before serging because your fabric is fed through slightly away from the knives to allow the stitches to hang off the edge. If you are flatlock seaming a loosely woven fabric that will ravel and could pull out during use, serge-finish the cut edges first with a narrow, medium-length, balanced stitch, using matching thread.

You may choose to have either the loops or the ladder side of a flatlock showing on the right side of your project (see Fig. 3-20). Both create a distinctive design detail. When flatlocking with decorative thread, keep in mind which part of your stitch will be exposed. Seaming with right sides together, the decorative thread must go through the eye of the *needle* if you want the ladder on the outside.

But if the loops will be on the outside, the decorative thread must be in the *lower looper* of a 2-thread flatlock and in the *upper looper* of a 3-thread flatlock. For additional details on decorative flatlocking, see Lesson 25 (page 117).

Reinforced flatlock seaming

We often use this durable flatlocked seaming method. First, straight-stitch the seam on your sewing machine. You may choose to serge-finish the edges before stitching. Fold on the seamline with wrong sides together if you want the loops to show. Fold with right sides together if you want to feature the ladder stitches. Using your widest stitch width, flatlock over the folded seam. Pull the stitching flat (Fig. 3-21). If you have not serge-finished the seam allowances, trim them close to the stitching.

Optional: Eliminate the straight stitching by pressing the seam allowances back and placing them together. Flatlock over the folds and pull flat. This also makes a durable flatlocked seam.

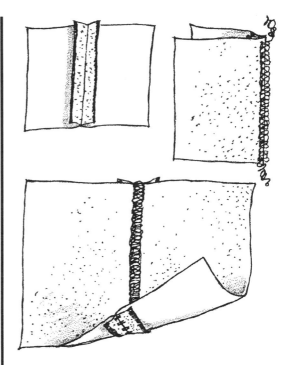

Fig. 3-21: For reinforced flatlocking, seam fabric. Fold and flatlock over seamline.

Test each fabric or combination of fabrics before you flatlock. You may need to adjust the tensions to accommodate the different thicknesses of your fabric. After flatlocking lace to tricot, for example, you may have to readjust your tensions before flatlock seaming two layers of tricot.

Project: Quick Slip

Whip up a pretty slip for any occasion with a length of tricot, two pieces of lace, and only three flatlocked seams. (Fig. 3-22)

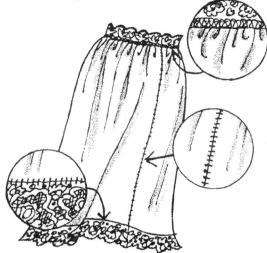

Fig. 3-22: *Use flatlock seaming to make a quick and easy slip.*

Stitch: 2- or 3-thread flatlock
Stitch length: Medium to long
Stitch width: Medium to wide
Thread: Matching color
    Needle: Serger or machine embroidery
    Upper looper: Serger or machine embroidery
    Lower looper: Serger or machine embroidery
Tension: Flatlock (needle thread loosened)
Needle: New, sharp size 11/75
Fabric: 1 fabric length of nylon tricot, as long as you want your slip
Notions: Stretch lace (at least 3/4" wide, with one flat edge)—to equal waist measurement; flat lace (with one flat edge)—to equal the slip bottom-edge measurement

1. Cut a fabric rectangle for the slip body. The length should equal the finished length desired minus the width of the flat lace. The width should be the hip measurement (measured 9" below the waist or at the widest part of the hip) plus 4". (Fig. 3-23)

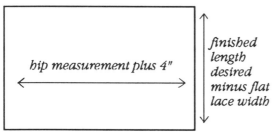

Fig. 3-23: Cut nylon tricot for slip.

2. You may want to serge-finish the upper and lower edges of the slip with a narrow balanced stitch and matching thread to stabilize them and prevent them from rolling while flatlocking.

3. Adjust to a 2-thread flatlock stitch. With right sides together, flatlock the flat lace to the bottom of the slip. Pull the seam flat. Notice that the 2-thread flatlock makes a very lightweight row of stitching.

4. Pull the stretch lace around your waist to a comfortable measurement (4" to 6" less than the waist measurement). Quartermark both the upper edge of the slip and the stretch lace. Match the markings. (The slip fabric is still flat, unseamed at the side.)

5. Change to a 3-thread flatlock. With the wrong sides together and the stretch lace on the top, flatlock the stretch lace to the slip, stretching the lace to fit. Avoid hitting the pins.

6. Using the 3-thread flatlock and with the right sides together, flatlock the side seam, matching the top and bottom laces. The less visible ladder stitches will show on the right side. Secure the seam ends by knotting the tails and trimming the remaining

4. Decorative Edges

Finishing edges is a basic serger function. In fact, it is the only way some home-sewers use the serger. But edge-finishing can go way beyond the basics. By making simple tension changes and using decorative thread, edges can become an ornamental element. It is important to consider the use of any finished garment or project when serge-finishing decoratively. If an edge will receive stress during use or wear, it must be stabilized in some way during construction or finishing. The stabilizing technique may be inconspicuous or decorative. Always test first with the thread and actual fabric you will be using.

When testing, look for stretching of the edges while serging. You may need to serge over a stabilizer such as elastic, cording, or decorative trim. Or serge over the fold of the fabric (see pages 61 and 74). Decorative serged binding (featured in Chapter 5) will also stabilize an edge.

Check to see if the decorative serged stitch will pull away from the edge easily. This is most common on chiffon and loosely woven or bias fabric. If so, you may need to lengthen or widen the stitch, try another kind of decorative edge, or save the fabric for another project.

Lesson 4. Balanced Decorative Edges

As soon as you've mastered tension adjustment, you're ready to embellish your garments and other projects with simple ornamental edges. If just the top edge will be exposed, use decorative thread in the upper looper only. If both sides of the serging will show, use decorative thread in both loopers. (Fig. 4-1)

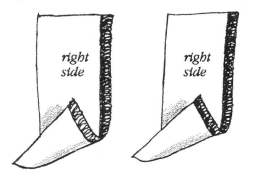

right side

right side

Fig. 4-1: *On a balanced edge, feature decorative thread in upper looper if only the right side will be exposed. When both sides will show, use it in both loopers.*

When decoratively serging curved edges, use a medium to narrow stitch width for easier handling and a neater stitch. If you plan to trim the edge while serge-finishing, clip away 2" of the seam allowance to the serger cutting line where you plan to begin and end the serging. (See the instructions for the hidden lapped serging technique, page 37.)

When serging outside corners, we usually simply serge off the fabric at each corner and then serge back onto the adjoining side. Most often, we secure the thread chain at each corner with seam sealant and clip the tail when dry. This method eliminates any pretrimming if your project seam allowances are wider than the finished serged stitch.

Serge-scalloped edge

Your sewing machine and serger can team up to create some unusual ornamental effects. If your sewing machine has a variety of decorative stitches, try different ones in combination with a serged edge. Most sewing machines have a blindhem stitch, which can be used to add a scalloped edge to your project. In testing, we have found that this stitch works best on a folded edge or two layers of light- or medium-weight fabric.

1. Serge-finish the edge. Use the same thread in both the upper and lower looper for ease in scalloping. To begin testing, adjust for a satin stitch length. The width of the stitch and the appearance of the scallops will vary with the weight of the fabric. Use your widest 3-thread stitch for medium- to heavy-weight fabrics and a narrower width for lightweight fabrics. (Fig. 4-2)

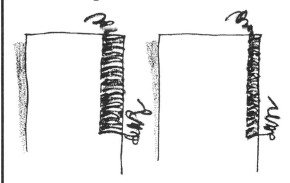

Fig. 4-2: *Use a wide stitch for medium to heavy fabrics. Use a narrower stitch for lightweight fabrics.*

2. Thread your sewing machine with thread matching the serged edge and adjust it for a blindhem stitch. Set the stitch width the same or slightly narrower than the serge-finished edge. With the serging to your left and the body of the fabric to your right, blindhem the edge, allowing the zigzag of the stitch to go off the edge to form a scallop. You may have to tighten the needle tension slightly to make the edge more scalloped. Adjust the stitch length to test different sizes of scallops before finishing the actual garment's edge. (Fig. 4-3)

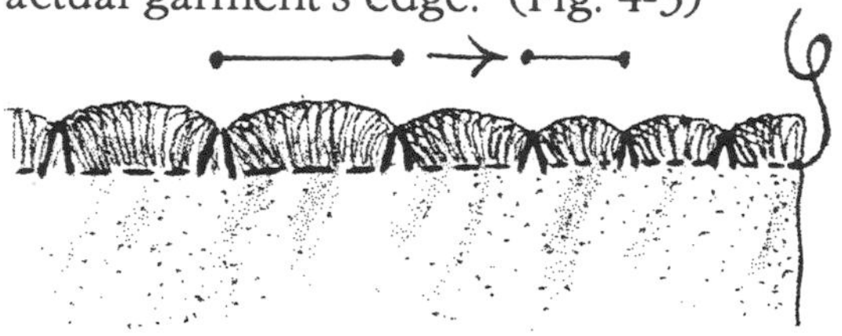

Fig. 4-3: *Test a length of sewing machine blindhem stitch to create desired size of scallop.*

Special Tip: When using the blindhem stitch to scallop the edge of a project, the bulk of the material must be fed through the machine to the right of the needle. To avoid this, use your machine's shell stitch (reversible blindhem stitch) if you have one. This will create the same stitch, but the bulk of the project remains to the left of the needle.

Serge-corded edge

Serging over filler cord (such as one or more strands of heavier thread, string, or cording) will stabilize a serged edge and add durability. The size of the filler cord or the number of strands used will change the thickness of the serged edge. When decorative thread and a satin stitch length are also used, the serge-corded edge becomes an attractive ornamental feature. (Fig. 4-4)

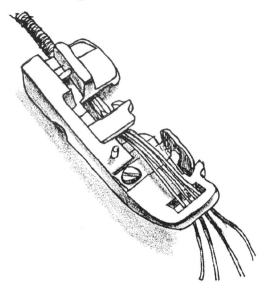

Fig. 4-4: *Serge over filler to create corded edge.*

When serging over filler cord, it is important to guide it carefully between the needle and the knife. The upper looper must go cleanly over the top of the filler, and the knife must not cut it. For even application, the filler is placed over the front of the presser foot and under the back.

We use several special tricks to keep the filler cord safely between the needle and the knife so that it will not be cut while serging. If your serger foot has an elastic/tape guide in the toe, thread the filler through the slots to guide the filler away from the knife.

If your serger has a metal component that screws onto the toe of the foot, remove it. Flip the component over and reattach it. (The screw is very shallow, so be careful not to lose it.) The component underside has a ledge next to the knife that will serve as a guide for your filler. (Fig. 4-5)

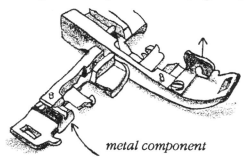

metal component

Fig. 4-5: *Unscrew and flip metal component (on some baby lock feet) to help guide filler away from knife.*

If the foot on your machine has a clear plastic component, use it as a guide without flipping it over. Loosen the screw to adjust the plastic piece so that it will accommodate the width of the filler. (Fig. 4-6) When the plastic component is extended, it also helps keep the fabric edge from curling.

Another trick to prevent cutting the cord is to use the knife cover plate to easily guide the filler cord. Place the end of the filler under the back of the foot and bring it over the front of the foot. Wrap it around the front of the knife, behind the knife cover, and out the side. (Fig. 4-7)

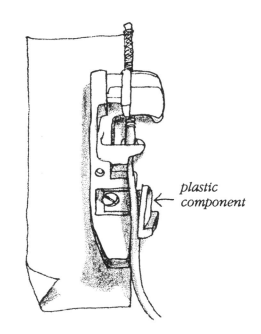

plastic component

Fig. 4-6: *Loosen screw and adjust plastic component (on some baby lock feet) to feed filler beside and under foot.*

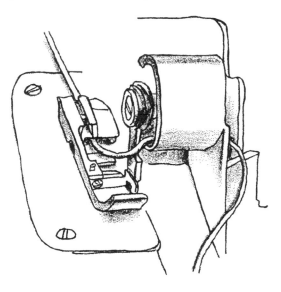

Fig. 4-7: *Guide filler behind cover plate and across front of knife to prevent cutting.*

Use several strands of matching-color filler cord for a thick, beefy serge-corded edge. Test by serging slowly over the strands to ensure that the upper looper will clear them easily. If not, remove one strand at a time until it does. Use a narrow balanced stitch and a short stitch length to replicate manufactured cording.

Allow several inches of the filler to extend at the beginning and end of the serging. To stabilize the edge, or when serge-cording around a curve, pull up on the filler to ease in the serged edge. Then knot securely. But remember, the rigid filler cord eliminates any stretch of the serged stitch.

For a cording that gives with the fabric as well as stabilizes, use elastic cording or 1/8" transparent elastic for filler. The elastics are especially good for serged filler cording on sweatering, interlocks, and other knits.

Project: Sunburst T-Shirt

Create a designer top by serge-decorating an inexpensive T-shirt. Have fun experimenting with different designs, thread types, and colors. (Fig. 4-8)

Stitch: 3-thread
Stitch length: Short (1mm to 2mm)
Stitch width: Narrow (2.5mm)
Thread: Contrasting color
    Needle: All-purpose or serger

Fig. 4-8: *Decorate T-shirt with narrow balanced stitching. Ruffle the seamlines by stretching as you serge.*

Upper looper: Woolly nylon
Lower looper: Woolly nylon
Tension: Balanced
Needle: Size 11/75
Fabric: Oversized T-shirt
Notions: Beads (optional)

1. Purchase an inexpensive oversized T-shirt from a discount store. Most come in packages of three at additional savings, so you won't have to make a big investment for your testing.

2. With an air-erasable marking pen, draw a simple sunburst design on the front of the T-shirt. To do this, make six lines extending 6" to 7" from the neckline seam. Two lines will begin about 3/4" on either side of the center front. Two additional lines on each side begin at the neckline approximately 1-1/2" and 3" past the first lines. (Fig. 4-9)

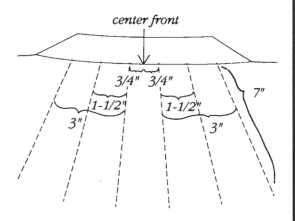

Fig. 4-9: Draw a sunburst design on T-shirt front with air-erasable marker.

3. With the wrong sides together, fold the T-shirt on each line. Starting at the neckline, serge over the folds to the end of marked lines. Stretch the knit to ruffle the fabric as you serge. To prevent cutting the folds, disengage the knife. Be sure to guide the folds so the looper threads meet exactly at the edge and do not stretch over the fold (for maximum thread coverage). Serge off the fabric at the end of each line and leave 4" to 6" of thread chain attached.

4. Using the same stitch adjustment and stretching as you sew, serge around the outer edge of the ribbed neckline. Start at one shoulder and end by serging approximately 1/2" over the beginning stitches, using the hidden lapped serging technique

(page 37). Raise the presser foot and needle and pull the T-shirt away from the presser foot. Clip the thread ends.

5. Fold the ribbing to the inside along the neckline seamline. With wrong sides together and the ribbing on top, begin serging over the fold, starting at one shoulder and stretching as you serge. (Fig. 4-10) Catch the ends of the sunburst lines in the stitching.

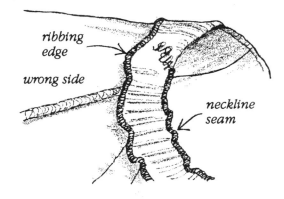

Fig. 4-10: After ruffling ribbing edge, fold ribbing to inside and serge over neckline seam.

Serge slowly when crossing the ends of the lines to allow maximum thread coverage. End by serging approximately 1/2" over the beginning stitches and pulling the top away from the presser foot as in step 4.

6. Repeat step 4 for the lower edge and sleeves. Start and end the lower-edge serging at one side seam. Start and end on the sleeves at the under-arm seam.

7. For a mock band effect at the lower edge, fold back 3" and pin with wrong sides together. Serge over the fold, stretching as you sew. Repeat for the sleeve edges, folding back 1-1/2" before serge-finishing.

8. Tie on decorative beads to the end of each sunburst thread chain if desired.

Lesson 5.
Rolled Edges

The narrow rolled edge makes a wonderful finish for most light- and medium-weight fabrics on any project from napkins to expensive dresses. With some adjustments, you also may be able to use a rolled edge on heavier fabrics. A rolled-edge finish may be either decorative or inconspicuous, depending upon the thread used. One of the original selling points of the home serger was its ability to do a rolled edge more neatly, quickly, and easily than a sewing machine.

The only visible thread in a correctly adjusted 3-thread rolled edge is the upper looper thread. (Fig. 4-11) When the tension is adjusted properly, the upper looper thread is pulled entirely around the edge of the fabric from needleline to needleline. The lower looper thread is tightened and forms a line that is almost straight. Both the lower looper and needle threads can barely be seen.

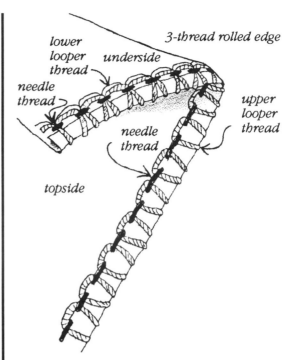

Fig. 4-11: *The upper looper thread wraps the edge. The lower looper and needle threads are barely visible.*

In a 2-thread rolled edge, the visible thread is the lower looper thread. (Fig. 4-12) It wraps the edge of the fabric from needleline to needleline much like the 3-thread version. For both types of rolled edge, you will need only one spool or cone of decorative thread.

With some decorative threads (and on certain fabrics), you may find it impossible to wrap the upper looper thread on a 3-thread rolled edge entirely around to the back using tension adjustment alone. One example is slick rayon thread. Use woolly nylon or monofilament nylon thread in the lower looper. The

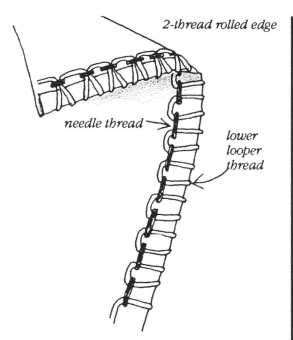

2-thread rolled edge

needle thread →

lower looper thread

Fig. 4-12: *The lower looper thread wraps the edge. The needle thread is barely visible.*

added strength of the nylon will help roll the edge completely. With monofilament nylon in the lower looper, loosen the tension before starting to serge. If the tension is too tight, the monofilament thread may snap. Because it is practically invisible, monofilament is more difficult to rethread.

To form a rolled-edge stitch, the fabric must roll completely around the needlelike stitch finger. If you don't cut the seam allowance portion wide enough to wrap around the stitch finger, short threads will poke out through the stitching. (Fig. 4-13)

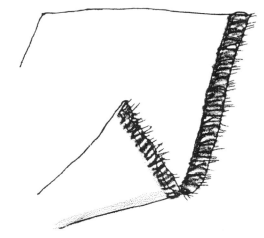

Fig. 4-13: *Threads may poke through the stitching on a rolled edge if the seam allowance is not wide enough to wrap to the underside.*

To eliminate this problem, adjust your machine for a wider stitch. If your serger has a plate that must be changed for a rolled edge, you must loosen the knife and move it slightly out. We find it is easy to start serging a rolled edge with the widest stitch width, then gradually narrow it as we test. With the built-in rolled-hem adjustment on the newer *baby lock* models, gradually narrowing to a proper adjustment is even easier.

If you still have threads poking through the stitching when using the widest bite, try shortening the stitch length to completely cover the edge with the serged stitches. Wiry fibers in your fabric or serging on the crosswise grain may also cause threads to poke through, but these problems are usually corrected by the same adjustments.

When serging loosely woven or lightweight fabrics, the rolled edge may pull away from the fabric. This occurs most often when serging with a short stitch length. If this happens, lengthen the stitch length slightly. You may have to widen the bite as well. The grainline of the fabric may also be a factor when the edge separates from the fabric. Test-serge on both the lengthwise and crosswise grains, as well as on the bias.

Lettucing

Lettucing the edge is a finish used only on fabric that will stretch, such as on knits and bias wovens. To make a ruffled lettuce edge, you must stretch while serging using a very short (satin) stitch length. (Fig. 4-14) Be

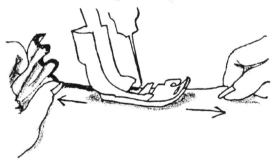

Fig. 4-14: Lettuce the edge of a stretch or bias fabric by stretching while serging.

careful not to bend the needle while stretching the fabric. If you have differential feed, adjust it to 0.7 to help with the stretching.

Because the fabric is stretched while serging, you may need to widen the bite to allow enough fabric to roll over the stitch finger.

Double rolled edge

Two rows of rolled edge serged directly next to each other make an unusual ornamental detail that is also very durable. Use two contrasting thread colors, or try two different thread types for a heightened effect.

1. Serge the wrong side of one edge of the fabric with a 3-thread satin rolled edge, leaving several inches of thread chain. Woolly nylon or a heavier rayon will provide the maximum thread coverage. (Fig. 4-15)

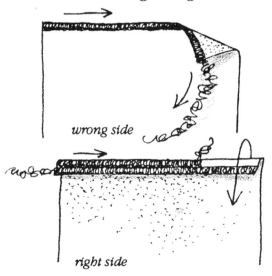

wrong side

right side

Fig. 4-15: Create a double rolled edge by serging one row from the wrong side. Then fold the stitching to the right side and serge the second row on the fold.

2. Rethread the upper looper with a contrasting thread.

3. With right sides together, refold the fabric next to the first rolled edge, leaving just enough width for another rolled-edge seam allowance.

4. Holding the thread chain to prevent jamming, serge a second rolled edge over the fold with the needle right next to the needleline of the original stitching. (Fig. 4-15) You will be serging in the opposite direction from the first serging.

5. Carefully press the double rolled edge flat.

Scalloped rolled edge

The scalloped rolled edge is similar to the scalloped edge made using balanced stitching (page 53). This edge finish is seen on the finest ready-to-wear lingerie. If you are using a scalloped rolled edge on nylon tricot, remember that tricot rolls to the right side. For the nicest rolled edge and the least frustration, serge the rolled edge from the wrong side.

Serge-a-fold

The rolled edge is a durable edge in itself. But if you prefer more body on the edge, or if you feel the serged edge may pull off a loosely woven fabric, press the edge 1/4" to the wrong side and serge the rolled edge over the fold. (Fig. 4-16) On the wrong side, trim the raw edge right next to the serging.

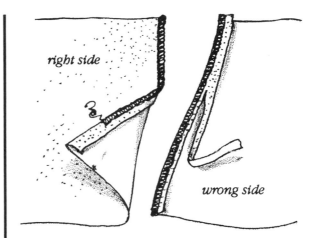

right side

wrong side

Fig. 4-16: *For durability, serge over a folded edge. Trim excess seam allowance on wrong side.*

For even more durability, combine serging on the fold with scalloped edging. If you are using a scalloped rolled edge on a single knit, the decorative stitch has a tendency to roll to the right side. To prevent this and add more body, serge-finish the edge with a narrow balanced stitch, press 1/4" to the wrong side, and serge over the fold. Finish with the blindhem stitch to create scallops.

Project: Christmas Tree Bags

These cute little Christmas tree bags are quick to make for gifts or decorating. The rolled edge stitch seams and finishes the bags in one step, leaving attractive thread chains for the handles. (Fig. 4-17)

Fig. 4-17: *Stow tiny gifts, candies, or holiday ornaments in these simple little tree bags. The rolled-edge seams and handles are serged all in one.*

Stitch: 2- or 3-thread
Stitch length: Short (rolled edge setting on 1)
Stitch width: Narrow (to roll the edge)
Thread: Contrasting color
  Needle: All-purpose or serger
  Upper looper: Heavier metallic thread, like *Candlelight*
  Lower looper: Monofilament nylon (same metallic thread for 2-thread)
Tension: Rolled edge
Needle: Size 11/75
Fabric: Scraps of Christmas fabric
Notions: 4 bells for each bag

1. Cut two 2-1/2" by 3" rectangles for each bag. With a cup or jar lid, round the two lower corners of each rectangle. (Fig. 4-18)

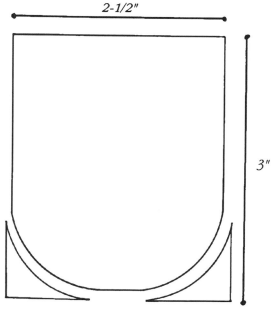

Fig. 4-18: *Cut two rectangles 2-1/2" by 3". Round the lower corners.*

2. Cut a side and bottom strip 8" long by 1-1/2" wide for each bag.

3. On the top of each rectangle and the short end of each strip, fold 1/4" to the wrong side and serge over the fold. Trim the fabric close to the stitching on the wrong side.

4. Serge the strip around the sides and bottom of one rectangle, with wrong sides together and the rectangle on the top. (Fig. 4-19) Leave

about 6" of thread chain on each end. Hold the thread chain taut to prevent jamming. When serging the curves, pull them around to meet the straight edge of the strip.

5. Repeat step 4 for the other rectangle.

6. Tie a bell to the end of each chain and knot the four chains together about 2" from the bells (see Fig. 4-17).

Lesson 6.
Tuck and Roll

The sewing professionals at Tacony were the first to show us this unusual decorative stitch. The tuck and roll is made using either a 4-thread overedge or a 4-thread mock safety stitch. The ornamental effect will differ depending on the stitch used. (Fig. 4-20)

Fig. 4-19: *Leaving a long thread chain, serge side strip to bag piece. Pull the strip around to meet curved edges.*

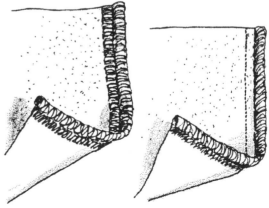

4-thread overedge   4-thread mock safety

Fig. 4-20: *The tuck-and-roll edge is created by serging a narrow rolled edge with a 4-thread stitch.*

It can be used on garments or other projects—anywhere you'd consider using a basic 3-thread rolled edge.

1. Adjust your serger for a narrow rolled-edge stitch (see page 58), but use both needles.

2. With a short stitch length, serge the edge. A tuck is formed to the right of both needles. You may want to use woolly nylon or monofilament nylon in the lower looper to pull the thread completely around the rolled fabric on the edge.

3. For a wider tuck and roll, adjust for a wide stitch using the same rolled-edge tension adjustments. The tuck will not be as pronounced in the wider stitch.

Project: Tuck-and-Roll Tablecloth

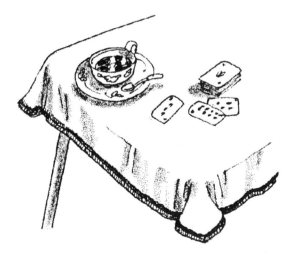

Fig. 4-21: A delicate tuck-and-roll edge finishes a tablecloth neatly.

A simple card-table cloth is the perfect place to feature the unusual tuck-and-roll stitch. Or change measurements for an elegant dresser scarf. Use plain or embellish with the serger cutwork in Lesson 37 (page 159). (Fig. 4-21)

Stitch: 4-thread overedge or 4-thread mock safety
Stitch length: Short (1mm to 2mm)
Stitch width: Narrow
Thread: Matching color
  Needles: All-purpose or serger
  Upper looper: Decorative, all-purpose, or serger
  Lower looper: All-purpose or serger
Tension: Narrow rolled edge
Needles: Size 11/75
Fabric: 54" by 54" square light-weight linen-like fabric

 Optional: Use a 14" by 54" rectangle of the same fabric for a dresser scarf.

1. Serge-finish all four edges with a narrow tuck-and-roll stitch. Serge on and off the fabric at each corner.

2. Secure the thread chains with seam sealant and clip the tails when dry.

3. If desired, finish the project with serger cutwork from Lesson 37 (page 159).

Lesson 7.
Picot Edges

The picot (or shell) edge is a version of the rolled edge and is most often used on soft fabric such as tricot. It finishes edges of lingerie garments and silky scarves beautifully. Simply alter a rolled-edge stitch (see page 58) for a long stitch length and a slightly tightened upper looper tension to make an attractive picot edge. (Fig. 4-22)

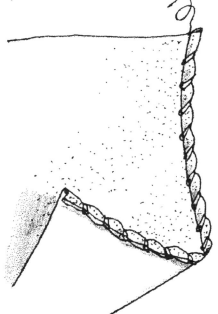

Fig. 4-22: A picot edge is serged by lengthening and slightly tightening the upper looper of a rolled-edge stitch.

Project: Pocket Scarf

A scrap of silky fabric and a simple picot rolled edge combine to make this pretty pocket accessory. (Fig. 4-23)

Fig. 4-23: A picot-edge pocket square is a simple serged project.

Stitch: 2- or 3-thread
Stitch length: Long (4mm to 5mm)
Stitch width: Narrow
Thread: Matching color
   Needle: All-purpose or serger
   Upper looper: Medium-weight rayon thread (3-thread)
   Lower looper: All-purpose or serger (3-thread) or medium-weight rayon (2-thread)
   Tension: Narrow rolled edge with upper looper tension tightened (3-thread) or lower looper tension tightened (2-thread)
Needle: Size 11/75
Fabric: 8" by 8" square silk or silky

1. Begin at one corner. Raise the presser foot and needle. Insert the fabric against the knife and just under the needle. Make two stitches by hand, turning the wheel to anchor the needle into the fabric.

2. Begin serging, holding the chain taut behind the presser foot and the fabric taut in front of it. Just skim the edge of the fabric with the knife. Serge off the opposite end.

3. Repeat steps 1 and 2 for the other three corners.

4. Secure the corners with seam sealant and clip the threads when dry. Tuck the scarf into a pocket.

Lesson 8.
Fishline Ruffles and Wire-Shaped Edges

The beautiful fishline ruffle was first adapted for the serger by a Tacony professional. Its ready-to-wear fore-runner is most often seen on special-occasion garments and floral-like embellishments. Fishline is applied to the edge of the fabric similarly to filler cord, using a short- to medium-length rolled-edge stitch. Wire-shaped edges are applied by the same method. (Fig. 4-24)

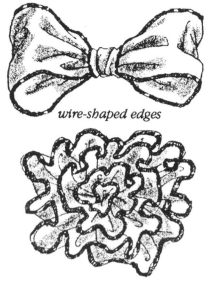

wire-shaped edges

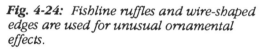

fishline ruffles

Fig. 4-24: *Fishline ruffles and wire-shaped edges are used for unusual ornamental effects.*

Fishline is available at most sporting goods, discount, and drug stores in weights varying from 12 lb. to 40 lb. The lighter weight is better for light-weight fabrics like tulle and netting. Use a medium weight (25 lb.) for fabrics such as satin and taffeta. Also use a heavier fishline if you are serging over two layers of fabric or if you want extra body. If you are edge-finishing a lightweight or sheer fabric such as tulle, be sure to use clear fishline.

Fine wire is available in any craft store. We first used lightweight floral wire to shape edges of serged flowers and for serged-wire ornaments. But most floral wire is precut to 18" lengths. Now we also use fine beading wire, which comes on spools and in a variety of weights and colors.

Serging on bias fabric creates the prettiest ruffles, but on a loosely woven fabric the stitching may pull off. As an alternative, cut the fabric on the lengthwise grain.

With both fishline and wire, it is important to guide accurately and **serge slowly**. If you accidentally cut the fishline or wire while serging over it, you'll need to rework part of your project. If you serge too fast, you may even hit the wire with a needle and throw your serger out of alignment. Fishline and wire projects are for more experienced serger users, and even they need to be very careful.

Both fishline and wire are placed under the back and over the front of the presser foot during serging (see serge-corded edges, page 54).

When serging over fishline, leave a long tail at the beginning and end of the serging (about half the ruffle length). First serge over the fishline for several inches, then place the fabric underneath. Do not stretch while serging. (Fig. 4-25) After serging, stretch for the amount of ruffling or flouncing desired.

When serging over wire, leave at least a 1" tail at both ends for securing.

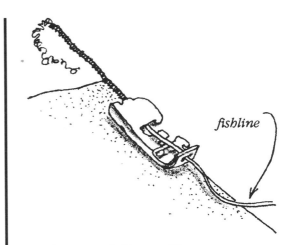

Fig. 4-25: *For fishline ruffles, serge over fishline, then stretch **after** serging.*

Begin by serging over the wire for at least one additional inch. Pull gently on the thread chain and the wire tail to guide the serging smoothly. Then raise the presser foot and position the fabric under the wire. Serge slowly. After some fabric clears the back of the presser foot, bend the wire back over the fabric to anchor it during the remainder of the serging. (Fig. 4-26)

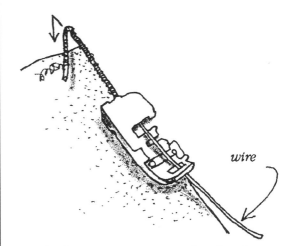

Fig. 4-26: *Start serging over wire, then insert fabric. Bend wire back over fabric to anchor.*

Project: Wind Twister

This colorful outdoor ornament is shaped by rolled-edge serging over wire on one long edge. It twists merrily as the breezes blow. (Fig. 4-27)

Fig. 4-27: *Wind twister with wire-shaped edges.*

Stitch: 2- or 3-thread
Stitch length: Short (1mm)
Stitch width: Narrow
Thread: Coordinating color
   Needle: All-purpose or serger

Upper looper: Woolly nylon
Lower looper: Woolly nylon
Tension: Rolled edge
Needle: Size 11/75
Fabric: 1/2 yard each of two colors 45"-wide water-repellent nylon, such as taffeta or *Ripstop*
Notions: 20-gauge beading wire (found in craft stores); one barrel swivel (from fishing supplies)

1. Using the pattern grid (Fig. 4-28), cut one twister and one 18" by 2" strip from each color of nylon.

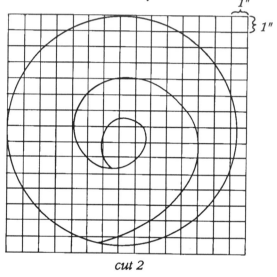

cut 2

Fig. 4-28: *Pattern grid for wind twister.*

2. Adjust for a rolled edge. Serge-finish the two long sides and one short end of each strip.

3. Serge the matching color strip to the narrow end of each nylon twister piece, right sides together.

4. Place the twister pieces wrong sides together and serge-finish the inner side of the circle.

5. Serge over 4" to 5" of wire, then insert the top of the twister and serge the wire to the outer edge of the twister circle stopping approximately 1" past the tail seamline. Then serge off the fabric but continue serging over the wire for another 6". Raise the presser foot and the needle, pull the wire back away from the presser foot, and serge off. Cut the wire leaving 12" past the end of the serging.

6. Smooth the fabric over the wire, beginning at the upper edge. Twist the lower end of the wire back on itself to secure. Clip away the excess wire. Attach the barrel swivel to the serged wire at the top of the twister.

7. Place the twister on a flat surface and flatten the wire into the original circle shape. Hang the twister from the barrel swivel.

Lesson 9.
Reversible-Edge Binding Stitch

The upper looper thread wraps the fabric edge to form the reversible-edge binding stitch. A narrow stitch works best for this edge finish because it allows the thread to cover the edge entirely. Similar to the rolled-edge stitch, reversible-edge binding is used on heavier fabrics so the edge does not roll under. Single-layer coats and blanket edges are common applications. Use heavier thread in the upper looper for a more durable edge.

Reversible-edge binding is formed

by loosening the upper looper tension and tightening the lower looper tension. The thread should completely wrap the edge and look the same on both the upper and under side. (Fig. 4-29) If the thread does not wrap completely after loosening the tension, narrow the stitch width. Or try taking it out of the first thread guide on your serger. Using strong woolly nylon in the lower looper may also help the stitch wrap completely.

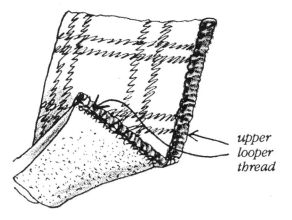

upper looper thread

Fig. 4-29: For reversible-edge binding, loosen the upper looper and tighten the lower looper. The upper looper thread should completely wrap the edge.

This simple but decorative edge finish is ideal for quilted fabrics used for place mats, potholders, or cozies. Before serging the edge of quilted fabric, compress the thickness by zigzagging over the seamline with a long wide stitch. Then serge directly over the zigzagging.

Project: Wool Lap Robe

The top of this 48" by 72" lap robe can be crazy-quilted from serged-together wool scraps. Or choose a soft wool yardage to complement your decor. (Fig. 4-30)

Fig. 4-30: Wool lap robe combines wool scraps with a flannel backing. The edge is finished with a reversible-edge binding stitch.

Stitch: 3-thread for decorative edge; 3- or 4-thread for serging patchwork

Stitch length: Short (1mm to 2mm) for binding; medium for serging patchwork

Stitch width: Narrow for binding; widest for serging patchwork

Thread: Contrasting or matching color

Needle(s): All-purpose or serger

Upper looper: Acrylic or cotton crochet thread for binding; serger thread for patchwork

Lower looper: All-purpose, serger, or woolly nylon

Tension: Tighten the lower looper and loosen the upper looper for the binding; balanced for serging patchwork

Needle(s): Size 14/90

Fabric: Wool scraps to make a 48" by 72" piece (or 2 yards of 54" or wider soft wool or acrylic) for the robe top; 2 yards of 54" or wider flannel for the backing

1. If you are using wool scraps, serge them together in any pattern to construct a piece measuring 48" by 72". (Fig. 4-31) Or cut the lap robe top from soft wool or acrylic to the same measurement. Cut a flannel backing piece measuring 48" by 72".

2. Adjust for a reversible-edge binding stitch.

3. With the wrong sides of the top and the backing together, serge both lengthwise edges. Then serge the crosswise edges.

4. Secure the thread chain on each corner by threading it back through the binding stitch using a darning needle or a loop turner.

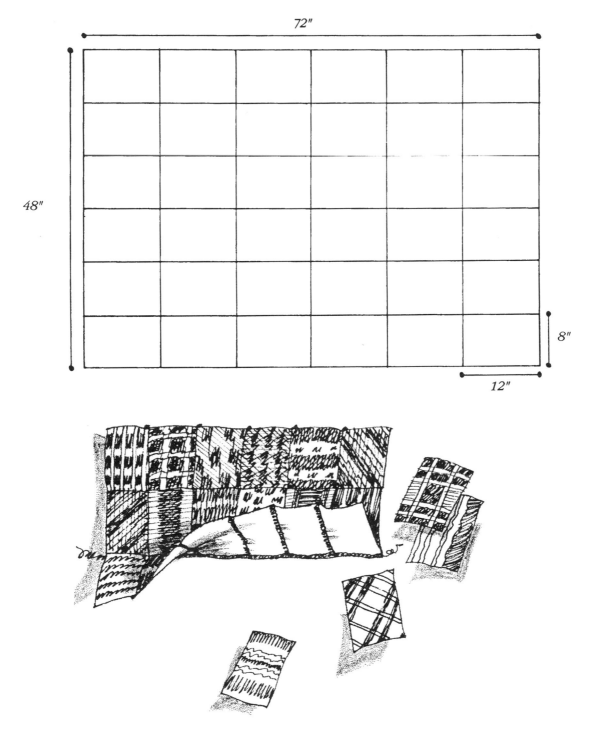

Fig. 4-31: *Serge together wool scraps for top of lap robe.*

Lesson 10. Reversible Needle-Wrap Stitch

Another decorative reversible stitch is the needle wrap, also called the blanket stitch. In this crochet-like edging, the needle thread wraps to the edge on both sides of the fabric, so the decorative thread used must be able to be threaded through the needle. The looper threads interlock at the edge of the fabric. (Fig. 4-32) Use the needle-wrap stitch as a decorative detail on an already-finished edge (such as a faced neckline or a hem foldline), or use it to finish edges on firmly woven fabric.

Either the 2-thread overedge or the 3-thread overlock stitch can be used for this edging. For the 2-thread stitch, loosen the needle tension and tighten the looper tension. For the 3-thread stitch, loosen the needle tension and tighten the upper and lower looper tensions so they interlock on the edge.

If you cannot loosen the needle thread enough by making a tension adjustment, narrow the stitch width or try removing the thread from the first thread guide on your serger. Using woolly nylon in the loopers can also help perfect this decorative stitch.

The look of a crocheted edge is most easily created by using a long stitch length. It also works best with the heaviest possible thread.

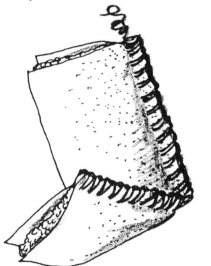

Fig. 4-32: *The reversible needle-wrap stitch shows a crochet-like edging by loosening needle tension and tightening looper tension.*

Project: Quick Potholder

Whip up a batch of simple washable potholders with reversible needle-wrap edging. You'll always have clean ones on hand, and they're great for gifts, too. (Fig. 4-33)

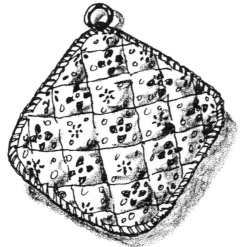

Fig. 4-33: *Speedy serged potholders are made by sandwiching insulating material between quilted fabric, then needle wrapping the edges.*

Stitch: 2- or 3-thread
Stitch length: Medium (3mm)
Stitch width: Narrow to medium
Thread: Contrasting color
  Needle: Buttonhole twist
  Upper looper: Woolly nylon
  Lower looper: Woolly nylon
Tension: Loosen the needle tension and tighten the looper(s) tension
Needle: Size 11/75 or 14/90
Fabric: 1/4 yard single-faced quilted, 1/4 yard insulating material, like *Thinsulate* or a *Teflon* ironing-board cover

1. Cut two 8" by 8" squares of the quilted fabric and one of the insulating fabric for each potholder.

2. Layer the quilted fabric with wrong sides together and sandwich the insulating fabric in between.

3. Round the corners using a small bowl or lid as a guide.

4. Zigzag around the edges to compress the quilted fabric.

5. Adjust your serger for a reversible needle-wrap stitch. If the needle thread will not wrap entirely by making tension adjustments or by removing a thread from a thread guide, narrow the stitch.

6. Starting in the middle of one straight side, serge around the edges using the needle-wrap stitch and just skimming the edges with the knives. Overlap the beginning stitching for about 1/2". Then raise the presser foot and needle, and pull the potholder away from the foot. Dab the ends with seam sealant and clip the tails when dry.

7. After serging, you may have to pull the needle thread to the right side with tweezers, especially on the corners, so the overlocking looper thread is right on the edge.

8. Hand-tack a round plastic curtain loop to one corner, if desired.

5. Decorative Trims and Bindings

Decorative trims and bindings can be serged directly onto the edge of your fabric, creating self-binding for craft and home decoration projects, as well as for garments from sporty to elegant. Trims and bindings can also be produced using a separate strip of fabric, which is then attached to your garment or project.

Many of the edge finishes you learned in Chapter 4 can be used separately or in combination to make a wide variety of ornamental trims and bindings. In addition to adding a unique decorative element, trims and bindings also help finish and stabilize project edges.

When applying edge-finishing or self binding directly to your fabric, always test first for stretching. If the area you will be finishing (especially a bias-woven or a cross-grain knit edge) stretches during the application, serge your trim onto a strip of fabric and bind the edge instead.

Lesson 11. Serged-Fold Self Braid

Many pretty edge finishes are not as stable as we may need for a particular project or fabric. In many cases, a neckline that is finished single-layer will stretch out. Or a single-layer sleeve edge on a loosely woven fabric may not hold up. With serged-fold self braid, the fabric edge is folded for more durability before serge-finishing. Heavy threads serged on the fold of heavy fabric can look similar to an actual braid trim. Lighter-weight threads serged on the fold of fine fabric give a more delicate, but stable, finish.

1. Press 1/2" to the wrong side. Turning less than a 1/2" allowance may be more difficult to keep a uniform edge.

2. Top-stitch 1/8" from the fold with a long stitch length. If your finished project edge will be visible from both sides, trim the allowance close to the top-stitching.

3. Put decorative thread in the upper looper and, if the underside will be seen, also use decorative thread in the lower looper. If only the right side will be exposed, you may use all-purpose or serger thread in the lower looper as well as in the needle.

4. Disengage the knife and serge over the folded edge with a short, narrow, and balanced 3-thread stitch. Use a blindhem foot or ornamental stitching guide for accuracy.

 Special Tips: If you are using heavy thread, lengthen the stitch to prevent jamming when you begin to serge. Too much thread coverage may also cause stretching or ruffling of the edge. If your model has differential feed, set it on 1.75 to ease in the edge (especially on bias edges). Always test first on project fabric scraps.

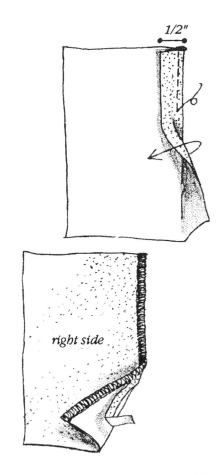

Fig. 5-1: *Create serged-fold self braid by pressing 1/2" to the wrong side, straight-stitching 1/8" from the fold, and serge-finishing. Trim the allowance to the stitching before serging if the wrong side will be visible; do this after serging if it will not.*

5. If you haven't previously trimmed the excess allowance, do so now. Use sharp embroidery or appliqué scissors and trim close to the serging. (Fig. 5-1)

To vary the serged-fold edge, adjust for a rolled-edge stitch (page 58) or a reversible-edge binding stitch (page 69).

For a more pronounced serged-fold self braid, serge over filler cord as discussed in Lesson 4 (page 54). (Fig. 5-2) For bias and curved areas, pull on the filler to ease the serged edge.

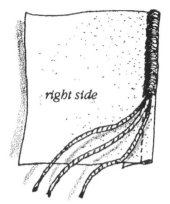

Fig. 5-2: *Serge over filler threads for more pronounced braid.*

Project: Lace-edged Handkerchief

Glossy serged-fold self braid and dainty lace finish the edge of this feminine handkerchief. Make four out of only 1/3 yard of fabric. (Fig. 5-3)

Fig. 5-3: *Lace-edged handkerchief with serged-fold braid edging.*

Stitch: 3-thread
Stitch length: Short (1mm to 2mm)
Stitch width: Narrow
Thread: Matching color
    Needle: All-purpose or serger
    Upper looper: Rayon
    Lower looper: All-purpose or serger
Tension: Balanced
Needle: Size 11/75
Fabric: 1/3 yard organdy or fine batiste
Notions: 1-1/4 yard 1/2"- to 1"-wide flat scalloped lace (with one straight edge) for each handkerchief

1. Cut an 11" by 11" square of fabric.

2. On two opposite edges, press 1/2" to the wrong side.

3. Top-stitch 1/8" from the fold. Trim the allowance close to the stitching.

4. Serge-finish both folds with a narrow, balanced, 3-thread stitch.

5. Repeat steps 2, 3, and 4 for both remaining edges.

6. Fold 1/2" of the lace to the wrong side at one end. Beginning 1" from one corner, lap the serge-finished handkerchief edge over the straight edge of the lace with the right sides up. Top-stitch along the edge of the serged-fold self braid, close to the needleline, catching the lace in the stitching.

7. Fold the lace at each corner to miter. When you reach the beginning of the lace trim, fold 1/2" to the right side and lap it 1/2" under the beginning lace before completing the top-stitching. (Fig. 5-4)

Fig. 5-4: Lap folded ends of the lace to finish handkerchief.

Lesson 12.
Quick-fused Self Braid

Another simple self-trim is created by serge-finishing garment or project edges from the wrong side using fusible thread in the lower looper. The serged edge is then folded to the right side and fused into position.

The width of the finish can vary by pressing additional fabric and the serged edge to the right side. For this variation, the wrong side of the fabric will show as part of the braid. There-

fore, the wrong side of the fabric must match or intentionally contrast with the right side. (Fig. 5-5)

1. Thread the serger with decorative thread in the upper looper, fusible thread in the lower looper, and all-purpose or serger thread in the needle.

2. From the wrong side, serge-finish the edge with a short, wide, and balanced 3-thread stitch.

3. Press the edge to the right side and fuse in place. If you are pressing more than the width of the serged stitch to the right side, cut out the project with a corresponding allowance for the extra fabric.

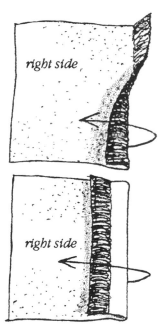

Fig. 5-5: For a thread-fused self braid, decoratively finish edge from wrong side with fusible thread in lower looper. Press stitching to right side and fuse next to edge or further over.

For a heavier braid, add a wide decorative finish over a narrow self braid.

1. Serge-finish the edge from the wrong side with a narrow, medium-length, and balanced 3-thread stitch with fusible thread in the lower looper.

2. Fold the stitched edge to the right side and fuse to secure.

3. Change to decorative thread in the lower looper and adjust your serger for a wide satin stitch. Serge over the narrow fused edge. (Fig. 5-6)

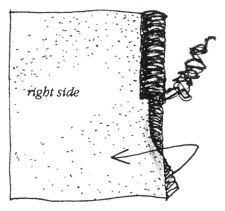

Fig. 5-6: For a heavier braid, make a narrow thread-fused self braid. Then serge over it with decorative thread and a wide stitch.

Project: Quickie Shoe Bags

The casing for these fast and easy shoe bags is decoratively finished with quick-fused self braid. The flannel fabric serves a double purpose: It keeps the shoes clean and buffs them at the same time—great for a business traveler. (Fig. 5-7)

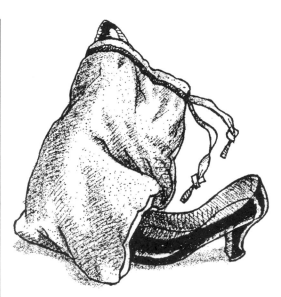

Fig. 5-7: Flannel shoe bags feature easy thread-fused self-braid casing.

Stitch: 3-thread
Stitch length: Short (2mm) for decorative; medium for serge-finishing
Stitch width: Widest
Thread: Contrasting color for decorative; matching for serge-finishing
Needle: All-purpose or serger
Upper looper: Crochet thread for decorative; all-purpose or serger for serge-finishing
Lower looper: Fusible thread for decorative; all-purpose or serger for serge-finishing
Tension: Balanced
Needle: Size 11/75
Fabric: 1/2 yard cotton flannel
Notions: 1 pair 27" shoelaces

1. For a pair of shoe bags, cut two 15" by 17" rectangles from the flannel.

2. From the wrong side, decoratively serge-finish one 15" edge on each piece for the upper casings (using crochet thread in the upper looper and fusible thread in the lower looper).

3. Rethread the upper and lower loopers with all-purpose or serger thread. Serge-finish the remaining three sides of both pieces.

4. Fold each bag lengthwise, right sides together, and straight-stitch the lower edge with a 1/4" seam allowance. Pivot at the corner and continue straight-stitching the side seam, ending 1" from the top edge. Backstitch to secure the stitching. (Fig. 5-8)

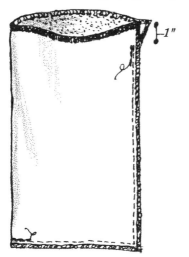

Fig. 5-8: Straight-stitch bottom and side of bag, leaving 1" unstitched at top edge.

5. On each bag, fold the decoratively serged edge 1" to the right side and carefully press to fuse the casing edge. Insert a shoelace into the casing and draw the bag closed.

Lesson 13. Serged Self-Binding

A simple self-binding technique uses part of the fabric to bind the edge. It is stable, as well as decorative, and can be a good option for a neckline facing or a center-front band. Self-binding is most often used on straight edges and stable woven fabrics, but it can be applied to curved areas on knit fabrics as well.

The width of the finished binding is determined by the width of the serged stitch. Use the widest stitch width possible on your serger. A 7.5mm stitch (available on several new *baby lock* models) with heavy-weight decorative thread makes the beefiest self-bound edge.

To make serged self-binding, add a 7/8" binding allowance to the pattern edge. Use a heavy decorative thread in the upper looper and all-purpose or serger thread in the needle(s) and lower looper.

1. With the wrong side up, serge-finish the edge.

2. Fold the serged edge 7/8" to the wrong side.

3. Rethread the upper looper with serger thread. From the wrong side of the garment, serge along the fold without cutting it. If the width of your stitch is narrower than 1/4", straight-stitch 1/4" from the serged edge. (Fig. 5-9)

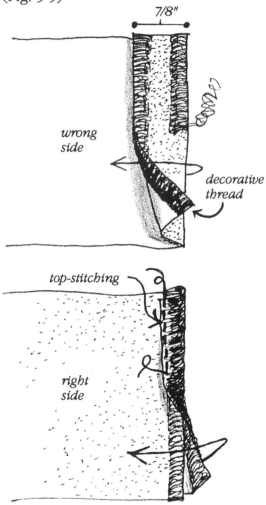

7/8"

wrong side

decorative thread

top-stitching

right side

Fig. 5-9: *Fold decorative edge to wrong side and serge over fold. Fold edge back to right side and top-stitch.*

4. Fold the decoratively serged edge to the right side (encasing the serged fold) and top-stitch.

Optional: Use fusible thread in the lower looper to add even more stability and elimi-nate the final top-stitching. Fuse to secure instead.

Project:
Canvas Tote Bag

Serged self-binding stabilizes and decoratively finishes the top of this easy-to-make tote. A 42" length of 36"-wide or wider fabric makes two bags. (Fig. 5-10)

Fig. 5-10: *Canvas tote bag sports serged self-binding and webbing straps.*

Stitch: 4-thread overedge or
  3-thread
Stitch length: Short (1mm to 2mm)
  for decorative; medium for seam-
  ing
Stitch width: Widest
Thread: Contrasting color for
  decorative; matching for
  seaming
  Needle(s): All-purpose or serger
  Upper looper: Cotton crochet
    thread for decorative; all-
    purpose or serger for serging
    fold and seaming
  Lower looper: All-purpose or
    serger (fusible thread optional)
Tension: Balanced
Needle(s): Size 14/90
Fabric: 1-1/6 yards heavy cotton
  canvas or cotton duck
Notions: 3 yards of 1"-wide cotton
  webbing (if you want straps long
  enough to fit over your shoulder,
  you'll need 3-3/4 yards)

1. Cut an 18" by 42" rectangle from
the fabric.

2. Apply serged self-braid to the two
short ends of the rectangle.

3. Fold the webbing into two equal
lengths for the straps.

4. Fold 1-2" to the wrong side on
each end of both straps. Place the
straps on the right side of the bag
piece 5-1/2" from each long side, as
shown. (Fig. 5-11) Butt the folded

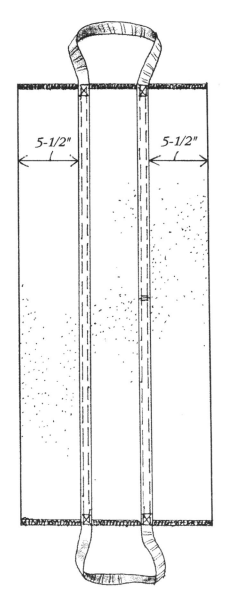

Fig. 5-11: *Position straps on bag. Top-stitch
edges. Reinforce with square boxes and cross
stitching.*

edges together in the middle of the bag piece and top-stitch the webbing on both sides to secure. Reinforce the handles at the top edges of the bag by top-stitching square boxes, then cross-stitch diagonally. The handles will be about 14", allowing the bag to be carried comfortably without dragging on the ground. If you purchase the longer webbing yardage to make a shoulder bag, the straps will be about 27".

5. With right sides together, fold the bag piece in half, matching the short ends. Serge-seam both sides, matching the binding at the top edge. If you used a 3-thread stitch, reinforce the seams with straight-stitching.

6. From the inside of the bag, fold the corners to points with the serging in the middle and straight-stitch a line 3" from the point, forming a triangle. (Fig. 5-12) This boxes the bottom of the bag.

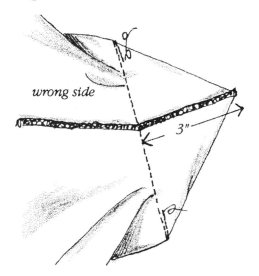

wrong side

3"

Fig. 5-12: *Straight-stitch inside corners at bottom of bag.*

7. At the top edge, press the seam allowances to one side and top-stitch parallel to the decorative stitching to reinforce and secure.

Lesson 14. Double-bound Edge

In Lesson 2 (page 43), you learned how to serge a double-bound seam. Fabric was folded over the seam allowances and then decoratively serge-finished. A similar technique is used to create a double-bound edge. Consider using it to trim garment edges or home decoration projects.

A double-bound edge can be serged either directly onto the fabric or onto a binding strip for later application. This edge takes a little more time (just like double-bound seams), but makes an attractive and durable trim.

1. Cut out the project leaving an extra 1" allowance for all edges that will be double-bound.

2. Fold or press 3/4" to the wrong side on each edge.

3. Adjust for your widest 4-thread overedge or 3-thread stitch and a very short, satin-stitch length. A 7.5mm stitch width will produce a binding more than 1/2" wide (twice the stitch width).

4. With decorative thread in the upper looper and the knife disengaged to prevent cutting the fabric, serge on the turned-back fold with the wrong side of the fabric on top. (Fig. 5-13)

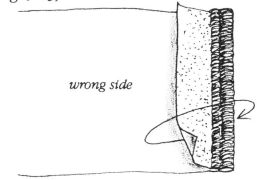

Fig. 5-13: Serge over fold from wrong side of fabric to begin double-bound edge. Fold stitching to right side and top-stitch.

5. Press the serged fold to the right side of the fabric and top-stitch to secure.

 Optional: Use fusible thread in the lower looper, then fuse to secure.

6. Fold the cut edge of the fabric toward the wrong side, forming a fold the exact width as your previous stitching.

7. Serge over the fold with the needleline on top of or right next to the needleline of the previous stitching. (Fig. 5-14)

8. If you are using a stitch narrower than 7.5mm, trim the excess allowance close to the stitching on the wrong side of the binding.

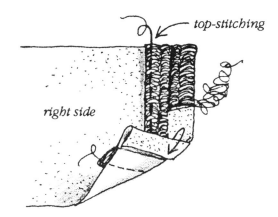

Fig. 5-14: Fold cut edge toward wrong side. Serge over fold, matching needlelines.

Project: Show-off Pillow

Double-bound edges accent a decorative inset piece on this fashionable pillow. We've embellished the contrasting inset fabric with diagonal rolled edges, but you may choose to show off any of your serger techniques. (Fig. 5-15)

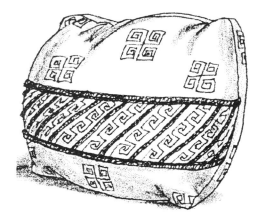

Fig. 5-15: Pillow with double-bound edges and decorative inset shows off serging skills.

Stitch: 4-thread overedge or 3-thread

Stitch length: Short (1mm to 2mm)

Stitch width: Widest for binding; narrow for rolled edge on inset; balanced for seaming

Thread: Contrasting color

Needles: All-purpose or serger

Upper looper: Woolly nylon

Lower looper: All-purpose or serger thread; woolly nylon or monofilament nylon for rolled edge

Tension: Balanced, rolled edge for inset

Needle(s): Size 11/75

Fabric: 1/2 yard of velveteen or similar fabric; 1/4 yard of contrasting fabric for inset

Notions: 16" polyester pillow form

1. From the pillow fabric, cut one 16" by 16" square for the pillow back. Cut one 5" by 16" rectangle and one 8" by 16" rectangle for the pillow front. If you are using velveteen, make sure to cut all pieces with the nap going in the same direction.

2. Serge a double-bound edge along one long edge of both pillow front pieces. (Refer to the instructions on page 82.)

3. From the inset fabric, cut one 9" by 20" rectangle. Press-mark evenly spaced diagonal lines about 2-1/2" apart.

4. Adjust for a rolled-edge stitch and serge over all the press-marked lines.

5. Carefully press the decorated fabric. Cut the inset piece to a 6" by 16" rectangle.

6. Overlap each double-bound edge 1/2" over the long edges of the inset. Top-stitch to secure, completing the pillow front.

7. With the pillow front and the pillow back right sides together, serge-seam the edges with a wide, medium-length, 3- or 4-thread balanced stitch. Leave an 8" opening at the lower edge to insert the pillow form. Turn right side out. After inserting the pillow form, edge-stitch or hand-tack the opening closed.

Lesson 15. Serged Piping

Traditionally, piping is made by tightly covering a cord with fabric, leaving a seam allowance for inserting the piping into a garment or project seam. We can easily replicate traditional piping by serging over filler cord onto a strip of 1-1/4"-wide bias tricot, such as *Seams Great*.

1. Thread the upper looper with decorative thread and adjust for a rolled edge with a short, satin-stitch length.

2. Serge over one or more strands of heavy thread or cording by placing the filler under the back and over the front of the presser foot. Refer back to Lesson 4 (page 54) for tips on serging over filler cord.

Special Tips: If your rolled edge is not completely wrapping to the under side, use monofilament nylon thread in the lower looper. You may need to increase the stitch width if you are serging over several strands of heavy thread or a thick cord.

3. Serge over the filler for several inches, then insert the bias tricot strip under the presser foot. Serge over the strip, trimming it about 1/2" with the knives. Do not stretch while serging. At the end, raise the presser foot and pull the filler tail to the left, away from the work, before serging off.

The filler cord itself may also be used as an ornamental element. Serge over decorative thread, ribbon, or braid using monofilament nylon in the upper looper and a longer stitch length. (Fig. 5-16)

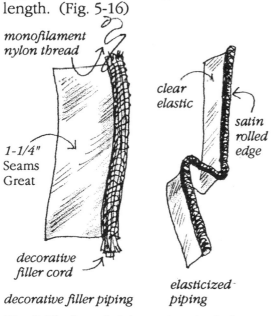

monofilament
nylon thread

clear
elastic

satin
rolled
edge

1-1/4"
Seams
Great

decorative
filler cord

decorative filler piping

elasticized
piping

Fig. 5-16: *Serged piping options include featuring the filler cord itself and stretchable piping.*

Create a stretchable serged piping for stretch and knit garments by using clear elastic in place of the bias tricot. Stretch the elastic slightly while serge-piping along one edge.

Finished piping is traditionally inserted in a garment or project seam using a straight-stitch and a zipper foot. New sewing machine piping or cording feet are now available to simplify the application. Also look for the introduction of serger cording feet, which will allow you to guide the piping and serge-finish the seam allowance in one simple step. Check with your local dealer from time to time and ask if any new accessories have become available for your machine.

Project: Serge-piped Book Cover

Cover your current paperback book with style. Serged piping accents the upper and lower edges. A matching satin rolled edge finishes the inner edges. (Fig. 5-17)

Fig. 5-17: *Make an easy paperback book cover featuring contrasting piping. Give one as a thoughtful gift or show it off yourself.*

Stitch: 3-thread for rolled-edge piping and trim; 3- or 4-thread for serge-finishing

Stitch length: Short (1mm to 2mm) for piping and trim; medium for serge-finishing

Stitch width: Narrow for piping and trim; wide for serge-finishing

Thread: Contrasting color
Needle(s): All-purpose or serger
Upper looper: #8 pearl cotton for piping and trim; all-purpose or serger for serge-finishing
Lower looper: Monofilament nylon for piping and trim; all-purpose or serger for serge-finishing

Filler: 4 strands of #5 pearl cotton, the same color as the upper looper thread

Tension: Rolled edge for piping and trim; balanced for serge-finishing

Needle(s): Size 14/90

Fabric: 1/4 yard denim

Notions: 2 yards of 1-1/4" *Seams Great*; 10" of 3/8"-wide ribbon to match the piping (for a book-mark)

1. Cut a 16-1/2" by 8" rectangle from the denim.

2. With matching thread and a wide balanced stitch, serge-finish both long edges.

3. With a satin-length, rolled-edge stitch and decorative thread in the upper looper, serge-finish both short ends of the rectangle.

4. Using the same stitch, serge over the four strands of #5 pearl cotton

onto the *Seams Great* to make at least 24" of serged piping.

5. For the upper edge, center an 11" section of piping along the 1/4" seamline on the right side of one long edge. (Fig. 5-18)

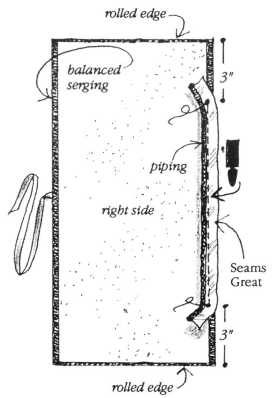

rolled edge

balanced serging

piping

right side

3"

Seams Great

3"

rolled edge

Fig. 5-18: Straight-stitch piping along 1/4" seamline, starting and ending 3" from each end.

6. Matching cut edges, pin one end of the ribbon on the wrong side at the center of the edge.

7. Using a zipper foot, straight-stitch next to the piping, starting and ending 3" from each end. You will have about 1" tails of serged piping extending past the stitching.

8. Repeat steps 5 and 7 for the lower edge. (Skip step 6.)

9. Fold 3" to the right side on each end. Matching the cut edges, straight-stitch over the piping stitching line, pulling the piping tails in the direction of the seam allowances at each corner. (Fig. 5-19)

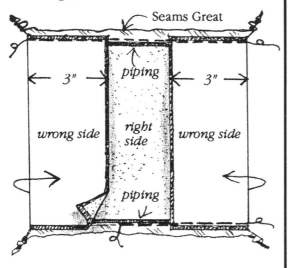

Fig. 5-19: Fold back cover pockets and stitch over piping stitching line. Piping tails are pulled to wrong side of seamline.

10. Trim the *Seams Great* close to the stitching. Turn the cover to the right side and top-stitch next to the piping along the upper and lower edges.

Lesson 16.
Mock Piping

Like serged piping, mock piping is made by covering filler cord with a satin rolled edge. It is not considered actual piping, however, because it is serged directly onto the fabric instead of being applied to a bias strip and inserted into a seam. We often see mock piping used as a decorative detail on lightweight robes, pajamas, and casual wear.

To create a simple mock-piped edge, serge along the seamline on the right side of the fabric using a satin rolled edge. Mock piping can be serged single layer on more stable fabrics or double-layer (wrong sides together). (Fig. 5-20)

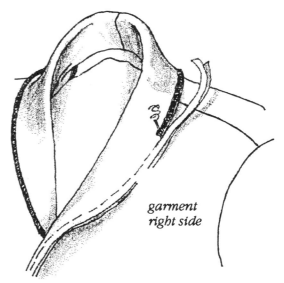

Fig. 5-20: Create mock piping by serge-finishing edges, wrong sides together, with a satin rolled edge.

On lightweight material, the fabric edge will roll inside the stitching, creating a piped appearance without filler cord. On heavier fabrics, it may not be possible to roll the edge. In this case, loosen the upper looper and adjust for a narrow, satin-length, reversible-edge binding stitch (page 69). Inserting filler cord will add to the piped effect.

A variation of the mock-piped edge is used to create mock-piped bands and cuffs on lightweight fabrics.

1. Fold the band or cuff lengthwise with wrong sides together.

2. Place the band to the wrong side of the fabric, matching the cut edges.

3. Serge mock piping with the band on top. (Fig. 5-21)

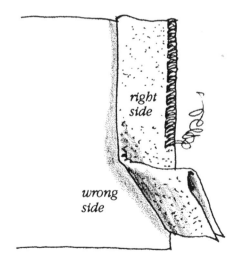

4. Pull the seam flat and press the allowances away from the band or cuff.

Another mock-piping variation can be used to hem sleeves and lower edges.

1. Lightly press 1/4" to the wrong side. Then press the hem allowance to the wrong side. This technique looks best with a hem allowance of 1" or more. If the hem allowance on your pattern is narrower, add a wider allowance when cutting out the project.

2. Make another fold to the wrong side equal to the hem allowance, sandwiching the 1/4" edge toward the inside of the fold, as shown. (Fig. 5-22)

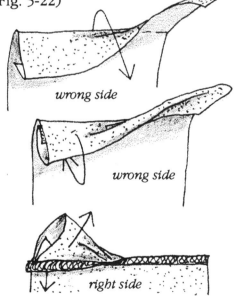

Fig. 5-21: *For mock piping, place wrong side of band against wrong side of fabric. Serge-seam with satin rolled edge.*

Fig. 5-22: *For a mock-piped hem, turn hem allowance to wrong side. Then fold again, guiding 1/4" of the first allowance toward the inside of the hem. Serge fold with satin rolled edge and pull seam flat.*

3. From the right side, serge over the fold with the satin rolled edge, being careful not to cut the fabric.

4. Pull the seam flat and press the allowances away from the folded hem edge. The cut edge will be encased inside the hem.

Project: Easy Mock-piped Apron

The bib and lower edge of this simple apron are decoratively hemmed with mock piping. The ties sport mock-piped edges. (Fig. 5-23)

Fig. 5-23: *Mock serged piping highlights hemlines and ties on this easy but serviceable apron.*

Stitch: 3-thread for mock piping and for serge-finishing

Stitch length: Short (1mm to 2mm) for mock piping; medium for serge-finishing

Stitch width: Narrow for mock piping; medium for serge-finishing

Thread: Contrasting color for mock piping; matching for serge-finishing

Needle: All-purpose or serger

Upper looper: Woolly nylon for mock piping; all-purpose or serger for serge-finishing

Lower looper: Woolly nylon or monofilament nylon for mock piping; all-purpose or serger for serge-finishing

Tension: Rolled edge for mock piping; balanced for serge-finishing

Needle: Size 11/75

Fabric: 1 yard 45" cotton/polyester woven

1. Cut one 14" by 17" rectangle and one 24" square for the apron. Cut two 30" by 3" and two 27" by 2" ties.

2. Adjust your serger for a balanced serge-finishing stitch.

3. Serge-finish the two long edges of the rectangle and three edges of the square.

4. Press each finished edge 1" to the wrong side and top-stitch 3/4" from the fold.

5. Fold each tie lengthwise with wrong sides together and serge-finish one short end.

6. Adjust your serger for mock piping. (See instructions on page 87.)

7. Finish the long and unfinished short edges of the ties with a mock-piped edge.

8. Hem the upper and lower edge of the bib and the lower edge of the apron using the mock-piped hem technique on page 88. The hem allowance is 2".

9. Lap the narrower ties 1" under the corners of the upper bib edge. Top-stitch in a square to secure. Lap and top-stitch the wider ties 1" under each corner of the upper edge of the apron. (Fig. 5-24)

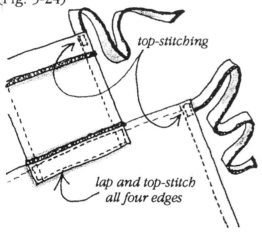

top-stitching

lap and top-stitch all four edges

Fig. 5-24: *Top-stitch ties to the apron. Lap bib over apron and top-stitch through all layers.*

10. Center and lap the bib over the upper edge of the apron, aligning the mock piping with the edge. Top-stitch all four edges of the lapped area.

Lesson 17. Serged Trim

It is often difficult to find just the right decorative trim for your fashion or project. Now you have a wide range of options for designing and serging your own. The base fabric width, content, and color can be varied. And you can use a large assortment of thread types and colors. Any decorative edging stitch is a possibility. Always test first.

1. Select a bias strip of woven fabric or a cross-grain strip of knit that matches or contrasts with the fabric that you are binding. Cut the length you'll need plus 1". The width of the bias strip should measure your desired finished trim width plus 1/2". For a 3/4"-wide trim, you'll need a strip 1-1/4" wide.

2. On one long edge, press 1/4" to the wrong side.

3. Adjust your serger for a balanced 3-thread stitch or any other decorative edge you'd like on your trim.

4. With decorative thread in the upper looper and the knife raised, serge along the fold.

 Special Tip: For easiest finishing, use fusible thread in the lower looper and a medium to wide balanced stitch.

5. Place the decorative side of the strip against the wrong side of the project fabric, aligning the cut edges.

6. Using all-purpose or serger thread,

serge the edge with a 1/4" seam. If your stitch is not that wide, serge-seam and straight-stitch at the 1/4" seamline. (Fig. 5-25)

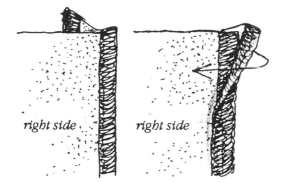

right side   *right side*

Fig. 5-25: *Decoratively serge binding strip. Serge-seam to fabric, then wrap decorative serging to right side and secure.*

7. Wrap the trim to the right side, encasing the seam.

8. Carefully press the trim in place and top-stitch to secure. If you've used fusible thread, carefully fuse the trim in place. Then top-stitching is optional but adds durability.

9. To add more texture or color to your trim, you may choose to use a wider binding and decoratively serge over the folded edge (without cutting it). Use a different stitch or stitch width for variety. (Fig. 5-26)

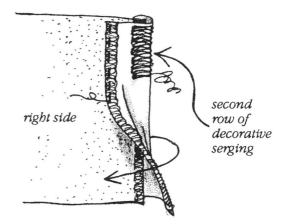

right side

second row of decorative serging

Fig. 5-26: *Add more color and texture to serged trim with wider binding. Then decoratively serge again after folding and securing binding on right side.*

Project: Serged-Trim Table Runner

Add elegance to a special dinner party with an easily constructed table runner. It is neatly serge-finished with narrow single-edged trim. (Fig. 5-27)

Fig. 5-27: *Metallic serged trim highlights an easy, yet elegant, table runner.*

Stitch: 3-thread for decorative; 3- or 4-thread for seaming

Stitch length: Short (1mm to 2mm) for decorative; medium for seaming

Stitch width: Widest

Thread: Contrasting color

    Needle(s): All-purpose or serger

    Upper looper: Metallic yarn for decorative; all-purpose or serger for seaming

    Lower looper: All-purpose, serger, or fusible thread for decorative; all-purpose or serger for seaming

Tension: Balanced

Needle(s): Size 14/75

Fabric: 2 yards tapestry or heavy brocade for 70" length (or 2-1/2 yards for 90" length); 1 yard matching lightweight satin for binding

1. Cut a 20" by 70" or 90" rectangle (depending on the measurements of your table) from the runner fabric.

2. Fold the fabric in half lengthwise. At each end, fold the corner back and press-mark a bias line. (Fig. 5-28) Cut on this line to form the end points.

3. Cut and splice 1-1/4"-wide bias strips of the matching lightweight satin to make a trim the length of the runner perimeter plus 1". On one long edge, carefully press 1/4" to the wrong side.

4. Adjust your serger for a short, wide, balanced stitch and decoratively serge the folded edge.

5. Along one side of the table runner (from point to point), serge the cut edge of the right side of the trim to the wrong side of the fabric. If your serger does not have a 1/4" seaming width, straight-stitch next to the serging on the 1/4" seamline. Wrap the serged-trim binding to the right side and top-stitch. (Fig. 5-29)

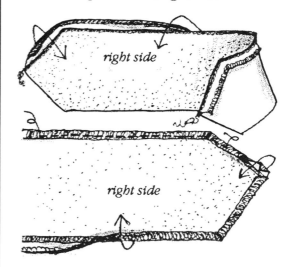

Fig. 5-29: *Apply serged-trim binding to one side of the runner. Serge seam opposite edge. Fold back corners to miter before top-stitching.*

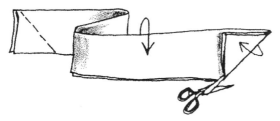

Fig. 5-28: *Fold fabric lengthwise, then align short edges back against folds and press-mark. Cut on press marks to form points.*

Optional: Use fusible thread in the lower looper of the decorative stitching and fuse instead of top-stitching.

6. Repeat step 5 for the opposite edge of the runner. Before wrapping the binding to the right side, fold back the corners on each end to form miters. Then top-stitch to secure.

7. Cover the end points and reinforce them with tassels by following the instructions in Lesson 35 (page 153).

Lesson 18.
Serge-piped Binding

A popular variation of the serged piping in Lesson 15 is constructed with a narrow rolled edge and a satin-stitch length. This binding gives the appearance of piping without the extra steps of inserting a piping strip. Serge-piped binding makes a pretty, delicate finish on lightweight or silky fabric—great for neckline and sleeve edges.

1. Cut a bias strip of woven fabric or a cross-grain strip of knit for the binding. Cut the length you'll need plus 1". The width of the bias strip should measure your desired finished trim width plus 3/4". For a 1/2" finished binding, cut the binding strips 1-1/4" wide.

2. On one long edge, press 1/4" to

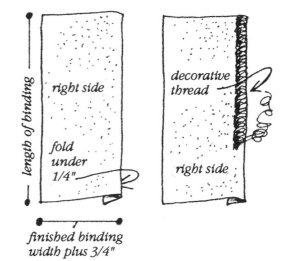

Fig. 5-30: *Make serge-piped binding by pressing 1/4" to wrong side and serging a rolled edge on the fold.*

the wrong side. (Fig. 5-30)

3. Serge-finish the fold with a narrow rolled edge, adjusted to a short, satin-stitch length. Use decorative thread in the upper looper and matching all-purpose or serger thread in the needle and lower looper. Shiny rayon thread is a good choice for silky fabric because it complements the fabric texture. To roll the edge completely with rayon thread, you may need to use woolly nylon thread in the lower looper. Test first.

4. Place the right side of the binding to the wrong side of the project fabric with cut edges matching.

5. Serge a 1/4" seam. If your widest serged stitch is narrower than 1/4", serge-seam and then straight-stitch at the 1/4" seamline. (Fig. 5-31)

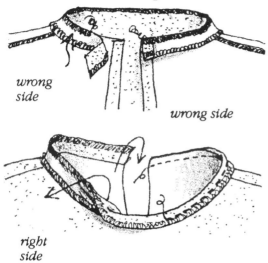

wrong side

wrong side

right side

Fig. 5-31: *Serge binding to wrong side of edge. Wrap to right side and straight stitch along rolled edge needleline.*

6. Fold the binding to the right side and straight-stitch on top of the rolled-edge needleline. Use a zipper foot to help position your stitches accurately.

Project: Padded Picture Frame

Serge-piped binding finishes the inside oval edge of this pretty 5" by 7" picture frame. Enlarge the measurements to fit a larger photo. (The binding is more difficult to apply if the size is smaller.) (Fig. 5-32)

Fig. 5-32: *Padded picture frame is trimmed with serge-piped binding.*

Stitch: 3-thread for decorative; 3-thread for serge-finishing
Stitch length: Satin for decorative; short (1mm to 2mm) for serge-finishing
Stitch width: Narrow
Thread: Contrasting color
    Needle(s): All-purpose or serger
    Upper looper: Rayon
    Lower looper: Woolly nylon
Tension: Rolled edge for decorative; balanced for finishing
Needle(s): Size 11/75
Fabric: 1/3 yard 45"-wide woven
Notions: 1/4 yard fusible transfer web; 8" by 10" polyester bonded batting; one file folder; 6" by 8" of 1/8"-thick cardboard; 5-3/4" by 7-3/4" clear acetate sheet (from school or office supply source); hot glue gun and glue

1. From the fabric, cut two 8" by 10" rectangles, one 6" by 8" rectangle, and one bias strip 1-1/4" by 18". From the transfer web, cut one 8" by 10" rectangle and one 5-1/2" by 7-1/2" rectangle.

2. To make the frame, cut a 6" by 8" rectangle from the file folder. Cut a 4" by 6" oval opening in the center of the rectangle, as shown. (Fig. 5-33)

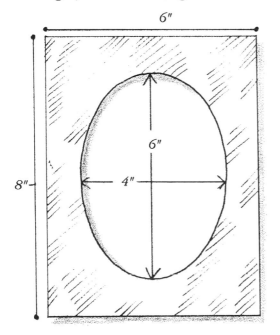

Fig. 5-33: From file folder, cut rectangle with oval in center.

3. Center and fuse together one 8" by 10" fabric piece, the 8" by 10" transfer web, the batting, the 5-1/2" by 7-1/2" transfer web, and the cardboard frame, as shown. (Fig. 5-34)

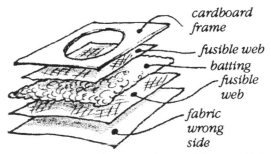

Fig. 5-34: Fuse layers to front of frame. Cut out along oval edge after fusing.

4. Cut out the batting and fabric inside the oval right at the opening edge. Fold the fused layers to the back of the frame on all four outer edges and glue in place.

5. For the binding, press 1/4" to the wrong side along one long edge of the bias strip. With decorative thread in the upper looper, serge-finish over the fold with a rolled-edge stitch. Serge about 6" of extra chain, leaving thread tails at the ends. The chain will be used for hanging the finished picture frame.

6. On one short end, fold the bias strip 3/8" to the wrong side. On the file-folder side, beginning at the lower right edge of the oval, place the right side of the folded end of the binding against the frame, matching the cut edges. Straight-stitch the binding to the frame around the oval opening using a 1/4" seam allowance. (You will be stitching through the file folder, as well as through the fabric and batting.) Lap the end of the strip over the beginning fold as you complete the seam. (Fig. 5-35)

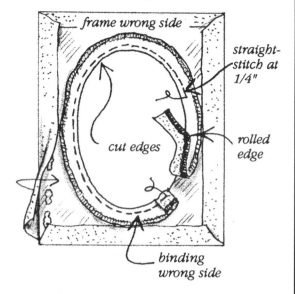

Fig. 5-35: *Sew right side of binding to wrong side of frame.*

7. Fold the binding evenly to the right side. Straight-stitch on the rolled-edge needleline to secure.

8. Make the frame back by folding the other 8" by 10" fabric piece over the heavier cardboard. Glue the edges in place.

9. With a narrow, balanced, 3-thread stitch, serge-finish the 6" by 8" fabric piece, trimming approximately 1/8" from all sides. Glue the serge-finished piece over the fabric edges on the cardboard back.

10. Use the rolled-edge chain made in step 5 for hanging. Hand-tack each end to the serge-finishing stitches on both sides of the frame back, about 2-1/2" down from the top edge.

11. Apply hot glue around two sides and the bottom on the front side of the covered cardboard and around all edges on the back side of the frame front. Keep the glue within 1/4" of the edge. Sandwich the clear acetate between the two glued pieces and apply pressure until dry. (Fig. 5-36)

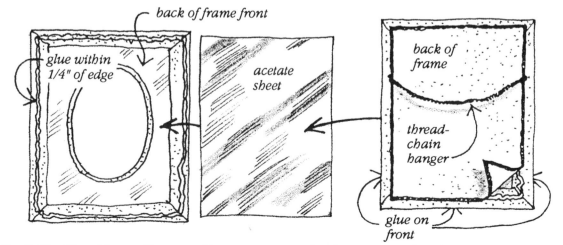

Fig. 5-36: *Glue sides and bottom of frame pieces, sandwiching acetate sheet between.*

12. The flower made in Lesson 24 (page 116) will cover the binding overlap and complete the frame.

Lesson 19.
Double Rolled-Edge Braid and Binding

The double rolled edge featured in Lesson 5 (page 60) can be adapted to make both a narrow braid and a decorative binding. Using contrasting thread colors for the two rolled edges will accent the delicate technique. Because maximum thread coverage and a perfectly rolled edge are important, we often choose woolly nylon for both the upper and lower loopers.

Double rolled-edge braid

To make double rolled-edge braid for trimming your garments, home decorations, or craft projects, serge over a 1/2" strip of base fabric. Choose any lightweight fabric that matches or blends with the upper looper thread color.

1. Adjust your serger for a satin rolled edge.

2. Serge one long edge of the fabric strip, leaving a thread chain several inches long.

3. Rethread the upper looper with a contrasting thread color. Serge the other side of the strip with the needle on or right next to the needleline of the original serging. (Fig. 5-37) Hold

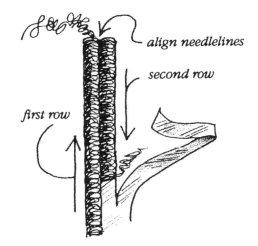

align needlelines

second row

first row

Fig. 5-37: *Make a double rolled-edge braid trim by serging two rows of rolled edging on a fabric strip, aligning the needlelines.*

the thread chain taut to start the serging without jamming. Aligning the needlelines and perfecting this technique may take a little practice.

4. Top-stitch the braid to your project fabric, stitching directly on the center needleline.

Double rolled-edge binding

A matching decorative binding is made by serge-finishing the folded edge of a bias-woven or a cross-grain knit binding strip using a double rolled-edge technique. Choose a lightweight fabric that matches or blends with the thread colors and the fabric to be bound.

1. Cut and splice the binding strip twice your finished binding width plus 1-1/2" by the length you'll need for your project. Fold the strip in half lengthwise with wrong sides together.

2. Serge, the fold with a satin rolled edge. From the wrong side, press the binding open.

3. Rethread the upper looper with a contrasting thread color. Then refold the binding strip and serge-finish the edge with the needlelines on top of, or right next to, each other. (Fig. 5-38)

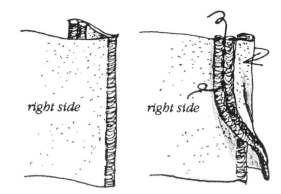

Fig. 5-39: Serge-seam double rolled-edge binding to edge of fabric. Wrap to right side and top-stitch on center needleline.

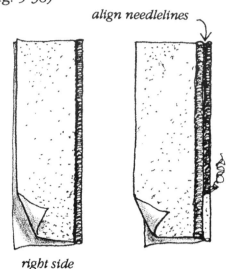

align needlelines

right side

Fig. 5-38: For double rolled-edge binding, serge-finish fold. Then refold and serge an adjoining rolled edge.

4. Place the right side of the binding to the wrong side of the fabric, matching the cut edges. Serge-seam with your widest stitch or straight-stitch a 1/4" seam. If you are applying the binding to an outside curve, ease the binding around the curve.

5. Press the binding to the right side and top-stitch between the rolled-edge rows to secure. (Fig. 5-39)

Project: Tooth Fairy Pillow

Double rolled-edge binding finishes the pocket and edges of this special little pillow. The tooth fairy will know just where to find the lost tooth and leave a reward. (Fig. 5-40)

Fig. 5-40: Special tooth fairy pillow is trimmed with double rolled-edge binding.

Stitch: 3-thread for decorative; 3- or
4-thread for seaming
Stitch length: Short (1mm) for
decorative; medium for seaming
Stitch width: Narrow for decorative;
medium for seaming
Thread: Contrasting colors
Needle(s): All-purpose or serger
Upper looper: Two contrasting
colors of woolly nylon for
decorative; all-purpose or
serger for seaming
Lower looper: Woolly nylon for
decorative; all-purpose or
serger for seaming
Tension: Rolled edge for decorative; balanced for seaming
Needle(s): Size 11/75
Fabric: 1/6 yard 45"-wide woven,
2-1/2" by 27" matching or contrasting bias strip
Notions: Approximately one hand-
ful of polyester fiberfill; 12" of
1/8"-wide ribbon for bow

1. Cut two 4-1/2" by 5-1/2" rectangles
for the pillow and one 4-1/2" by 3-1/2"
rectangle for the pocket. Place the
pocket over the two pillow pieces and
match the cut edges at one end.
Using a cup, round all four corners.
(Fig. 5-41)

2. Make double rolled-edge binding
on the bias strip following the instructions on pages 97 and 98. Trim the
strip width to 1".

3. Bind the upper (straight) edge of
the pocket by applying the right side
of the binding to the wrong side of the
pocket. Wrap the binding to the right
side and top-stitch on the rolled-edge
needleline.

Fig. 5-41: *Place smaller rectangle over two
larger rectangles and round corners.*

4. Place the pillow pieces wrong
sides together with the pocket on the
top, matching the cut edges. Serge-
seam around the pillow with a medium-width (3mm to 3.5mm) balanced
stitch. Leave an opening at the top for
inserting the fiberfill. Stuff the pillow
and serge-seam the opening closed.

5. On one short end, fold the binding
strip 1/2" to the wrong side. Beginning in the middle of the top edge,
place the right side of the folded end
of the binding against the wrong side
of the pillow, matching the cut edges.
Serge with a 1/4" seam allowance,
lapping the end of the strip over the
beginning fold as you complete the
seam. If your serger does not have a
stitch that wide, straight-stitch on the
1/4" seamline after serging.

6. Fold the binding to the right side and top-stitch on the rolled-edge needleline to secure.

7. Add a bow at the top of the pillow to cover the binding joint.

Lesson 20. Elasticized Trims and Binding

The serger makes sewing stretch and knit fabrics a breeze. Now you can also serge elasticized trims and binding to add decorative detail and to individualize your garments.

Elasticized trims

A classic example of new products leading to new techniques, serging elasticized trim was rarely considered before the introduction of clear elastic. Now we can make a variety of stretch trims to coordinate with any stretch or knit fabric. Different stitch widths, tension adjustments, and thread types add to the possibilities.

Because clear elastic is so lightweight, it is important to serge through it to keep it from rolling. Neatly trim the excess elastic after serging the trim.

Single-stretch Trim

1. Begin with a single row of serging on a piece of clear elastic. Test various widths.

2. Adjust the stitch width to the width of braid desired. The elastic width must be wider than the stitch width.

3. Serge, using a short (not satin) 2mm stitch length. For better coverage, use woolly nylon in both loopers.

4. Adjust the tension for a balanced 3-thread stitch, making it loose enough to allow the elastic to lie flat. After serging several inches, test the braid by stretching. If the stitches break, loosen the needle thread tension or stretch the elastic slightly.

5. Hold the elastic taut in front of and behind the presser foot while serging. It is not necessary to stretch because the serged stitch allows for stretch.

6. Trim the elastic close to the serging, being careful not to cut the stitches. (Fig. 5-42) If part of the elastic still remains, it won't show when the trim is top-stitched to the garment.

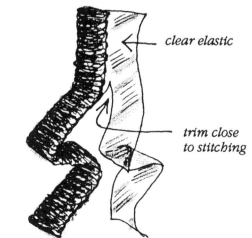

clear elastic

trim close to stitching

Fig. 5-42: *Decoratively serge clear elastic, then trim close to stitching to make single-stretch trim.*

7. Top-stitch the trim to the garment using a long stitch and sewing close to each edge of the trim. Stretch the elastic as you sew.

Double-stretch Trim

Select an elastic that is wider than the trim you'll be making.

1. Serge one side of the elastic following the above guidelines, except do not trim the elastic.

2. On the opposite (unserged) side, serge another row with the needle just inside or next to the needleline of the previous stitching. (Fig. 5-43) For

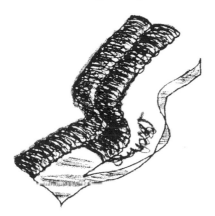

Fig. 5-43: Double-stretch trim features a second row of serging with needlelines aligned.

variation, use a different thread color in the upper looper when serging the second side.

3. Top-stitch the trim to the garment using a long stitch and sewing close to each edge of the trim. Stretch the elastic as you sew.

Stretch Trim Variations

Adjust your serger for a narrow (2mm to 3mm), balanced stitch. Tighten the lower looper tension slightly. Serge the elastic, following the directions for the double-stretch trim above.

Try serging a balanced stitch on one side and a rolled-edge stitch on the other side. Or serge a rolled edge on both sides, overlapping the needlelines. (Fig. 5-44) For more

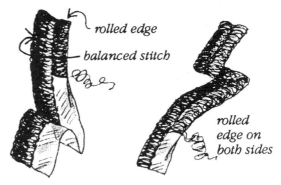

Fig. 5-44: Stretch trim variations include double trim with one or two rolled edges.

elasticity when serging a rolled edge on clear elastic, stretch the elastic. It will return to its original length after serging.

Braided Trim

Braid elastic trim for swimsuit or camisole straps:

1. Serge a strand of single-stretch trim six times the length of the strap plus 6".

2. Cut the trim into six equal lengths. Braid it into two straps and secure the ends with straight-stitching. (Fig. 5-45)

Fig. 5-45: *Braided stretch trim is used for swimsuit and camisole straps.*

3. Attach the straps to your garment according to the pattern guidesheet.

Elasticized binding

This technique adds stretch and stability to an edge and creates a neat, decorative binding at the same time. You have the option of leaving one serged-finished edge exposed on the under side of the binding or wrapping and twin-needle top-stitching to leave no serged edges exposed.

Elasticized binding works especially well on stretch fabrics because the serged stitch used to apply the elastic is a stretch stitch. Use it to finish the edges of swim or exercisewear. You can even extend the binding past the garment edge to form straps.

Any width elastic may be used, but 3/8" is most versatile. Select any type except clear elastic. (It will roll inside the binding.)

To bind the edge of stretch fabric:

1. Cut the elastic to the desired length. Cut a stretch binding strip the same length. Its width should be three times the width of the elastic plus 1/4". For a heavy or thick fabric, cut the strip an additional 1/4" wider.

2. Serge-finish one long edge of the strip using a medium width and length 3-thread stitch, trimming only slightly to neaten.

3. Place the right sides of the binding and fabric together, matching the cut edges. Straight-stitch with a seam allowance the width of the elastic (usually 3/8"). Stretch the layers as you sew. (Fig. 5-46)

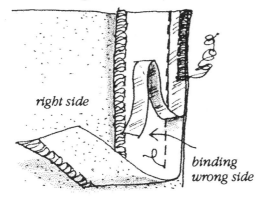

Fig. 5-46: *For elasticized binding, straight-stitch trim to garment, stretching both layers. Serge elastic to seam allowance on top of trim.*

4. Adjust the serger for a long, balanced, 3-thread stitch. Place the elastic on top of the trim, next to the edge. Serge it to the seam allowance through all layers.

5. Fold the binding to the wrong side, encasing the serged seam allowance. From the right side, top-stitch on the binding with a narrow zigzag or a twin needle to secure, stretching slightly as you sew. (Fig. 5-47) Or stitch-in-the-ditch from the right side, stretching firmly.

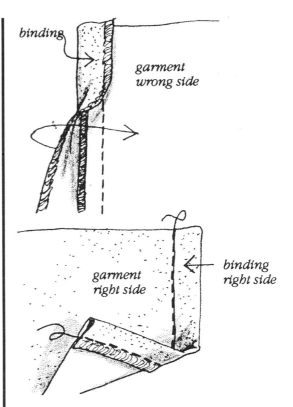

Fig. 5-47: *Fold binding to wrong side and top-stitch or stitch-in-the-ditch.*

Optional: To make a binding with no exposed serging, the width of the binding strip should be four times the width of the elastic plus 1/4". Don't serge-finish one long edge. After applying (steps 3 and 4), fold the unsewn edge of the binding 3/8" (the width of the seam allowance) to the wrong side, matching the cut edge to the serged edge.

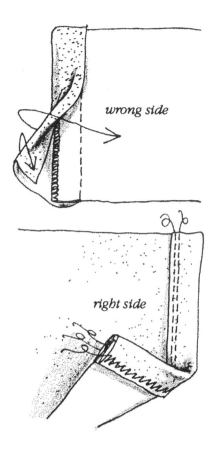

Fig. 5-48: For unfinished elasticized binding, fold unsewn edge to wrong side. Top-stitch or stitch-in-the-ditch to secure.

Fold 3/8" again, encasing the serged elastic. From the right side, top-stitch as above. (Fig. 5-48)

The application of elasticized binding varies slightly from stretch fabrics to wovens. When applying elasticized binding to the edge of woven fabric, the fabric is gathered in with the elastic, so it must be cut larger than the opening.

1. Cut the elastic smaller than the opening, to the desired length.

2. If you are applying the binding to a curved area, cut the trim strip on the bias to allow it to lie smoothly.

3. Straight-stitch the binding to the fabric without stretching.

4. When applying the elastic, stretch the elastic to fit the length of the binding as you serge.

5. Finish as instructed for the stretch binding.

Project: Ruffled Jar Cover

Serged elastic trim tucks this decorative cover around any jar lid. A ribbon bow adds a pretty finishing touch. (Fig. 5-49)

Fig. 5-49: Ruffled jar cover has serged clear-elastic trim.

Stitch: 3-thread
Stitch length: Short
Stitch width: Narrow
Thread: Contrasting color
    Needle: All-purpose or serger
    Upper looper: Woolly nylon
    Lower looper: All-purpose or
       serger
Tension: Balanced for braid trim;
    rolled edge for serge-finishing
Needle: Size 11/75
Fabric: 1/4 yard gingham (or 8" by
    8" square)
Notions: 12" of 1/4"- or 3/8"-wide
    clear elastic; 12" of 1/8"-wide
    ribbon; air-erasable marker

1. Cut an 8" circle from the gingham, using a lid or plate as a guide. With a smaller lid, mark a 5-1/2" circle inside the larger one using an air-erasable marker.

2. Serge-finish the edge of the larger circle with a rolled edge.

3. Serge along one edge of the elastic with a narrow satin stitch. Trim the unsewn elastic close to the serging.

4. Pin-mark the inner circle in halves and the elastic trim at 3-1/2" and 7". Place the elastic on the circle and straight-stitch through it with a long stitch, stretching to fit the markings. (Fig. 5-50) Finish by lapping the end over the beginning of the trim.

5. Tie the ribbon into a bow and hand-tack it over the joined ends of the elastic.

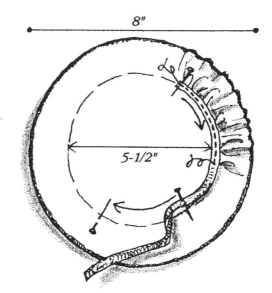

Fig. 5-50: *Stretch clear elastic trim while top-stitching.*

Lesson 21.
Puffed Serged Braid

A thread chain serged from heavy decorative thread can be used as ornamental braid. Serging over several strands of filler (as described in previous lessons) makes a heavier braid. For an even chunkier, puffed braid, serge over rolled fabric or thick yarn.

A strip of 1"-wide tricot, T-shirt knit, or jersey (cut on the crosswise grain) can be used for the puff-braid filler. Or use 5/8"-wide *Seams Great* for a more delicate braid. When pulled, the fabric strip rolls into a narrow tube and serger stitches can be formed around it. The resulting puffed braid is ideal for edging, couching, and craft projects.

Use decorative thread in the upper and lower looper with matching all-purpose or serger thread in the needle. Use heavier decorative thread when serging over thicker fabric such as jersey; use finer thread for serging over lightweight filler.

1. Pull the fabric strip slightly so that it rolls into a tube.

2. Place the tube under the back of the presser foot and over the front, between the needle and the knives. Allow approximately an inch of the tube to extend in back of the presser foot.

3. Hold the end of the tube taut behind the foot to prevent jamming as you begin to serge.

4. Continue to hold the serged braid taut (but **don't** pull), guiding it smoothly out the back of the foot. The stitches should form around, and not through, the tube. (Fig. 5-51)

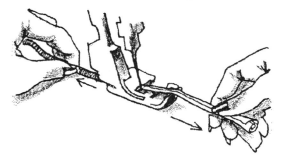

Fig. 5-51: *Make puffed serged braid by serging around a fabric tube or chunky yarn.*

Puffed serged braid may be tacked to your fabric to form a letter or design. Twist or braid strands together for a more pronounced trim. (Fig. 5-52)

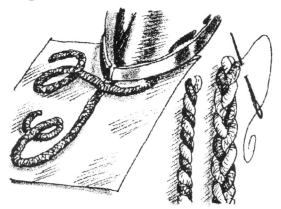

Fig. 5-52: *Puffed serged braid can be tacked or fused to fabric to form letters or designs. Twist or braid multiple strands for pronounced effect.*

Special Tip: Use fusible thread in the lower looper to create fusible puffed braid. In most instances, the fusible thread will permanently bond the braid in place. For more durability, hand-tack it to the fabric, catching only the backside of the braid.

Project: Frog Closures

Heavy rayon thread is serged over a tube of wool jersey, then easily formed into traditional frog closures. Use two on the fringed scarf in Lesson 26 (page 123) or embellish your latest fashion garment. (Fig. 5-53)

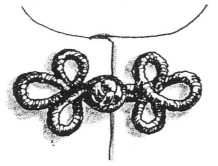

Fig. 5-53: Make your own decorative frog closures with puffed serged braid.

Stitch: 3-thread
Stitch length: Medium (2.5mm to 3mm)
Stitch width: Medium to wide (5mm)
Thread· Matching color
   Needle: All-purpose or serger
   Upper looper: Heavy rayon, like *Decor 6* or pearl rayon
   Lower looper: Woolly nylon
Tension: Balanced, with lower looper slightly tightened
Needle: Size 11/75
Fabric: Two 1" strips of 60"-wide wool or acrylic jersey, cut on the crosswise grain

1. Create puff braid from the 60" jersey strips, following the instructions on page 106.

2. Cut two 10-1/2" strips and two 22" strips of the braid. Apply seam sealant to each end.

3. From the short strips, form decorative loops, as shown. (Fig. 5-54) Hand-tack the braid together from the wrong side.

Fig. 5-54: Form looped side of closure and hand-tack.

4. Using the longer strips, make a button with decorative loops matching those above. (Fig. 5-55) Hand-tack the braid together from the wrong side.

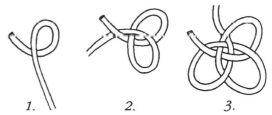

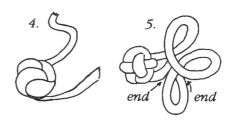

Fig. 5-55: Make ball button, then form the tail into three decorative loops.

Lesson 22.
Serged Ribbon Trim and Binding

The bindings and trims in previous lessons have been serged onto fabric. Another option for trimming and binding straight edges is to decoratively serge purchased ribbon before applying it to your project fabric. Serged ribbon can be used on craft and accessory projects, as well as on garment edges. Apply it down the front of a blouse or sweater or as a tuxedo stripe down pantlegs.

Either top-stitch the ribbon trim in place or use it as a binding. Lap the right side of the ribbon over the wrong-side edge of the fabric and top-stitch. (Fig. 5-56) Turn the ribbon to the right side of the fabric and top-stitch the opposite edge in place, as shown.

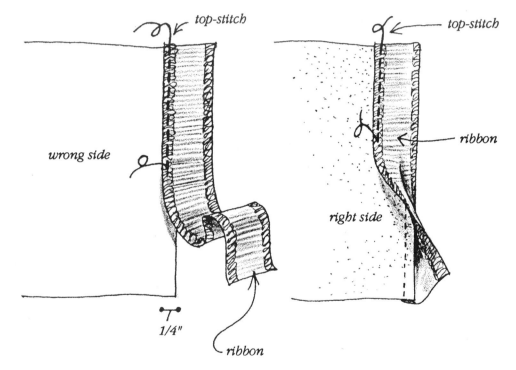

Fig. 5-56: *Top-stitch serged ribbon to fabric edge. Then turn the ribbon to the right side and top-stitch again to bind edge.*

Project: Ribbon Sampler Bookmark

Feature a variety of serged stitches on your pretty ribbon bookmark. Then use a spray or dip-type stiffener to preserve the results. (Fig. 5-57)

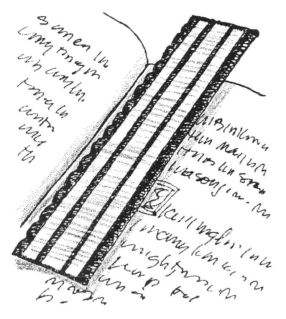

Fig. 5-57: *The ribbon sampler bookmark features five edge finishes.*

Stitch: 3-thread
Stitch length: Short (1mm)
Stitch width: Varies with stitch
Thread: Contrasting color
   Needle: All-purpose or serger
   Upper looper: Woolly nylon
   Lower looper: Woolly nylon
Tension: Varies with stitch
Needle: Size 11/75
Fabric: 10" of 1-1/2"-wide soft
   ribbon (vary the length for larger
   or smaller books)

1. Press-mark two lengthwise lines down the center of the ribbon, dividing it into vertical thirds.

2. Adjust for a satin-length narrow rolled edge and serge along one fold.

3. Change to a satin-length, narrow, and balanced stitch and serge along the other fold.

4. Widen your stitch and satin-serge both short ends and one long edge.

5. Scallop the finished long edge with a sewing machine blindhem stitch. Use a wide stitch width and allow the zigzag to stitch off the edge. You may need to tighten the needle tension slightly to pull up the scallop. (See page 53.)

6. Adjust for a reversible needle-wrap stitch (Lesson 10, page 72) by loosening the upper looper and tightening the lower looper. Serge the remaining ribbon edge.

7. Spray or dip the bookmark in a stiffening solution, such as *Stiffy* or *TAC Spray Stiff*. Clip any thread tails when dry.

6. Special Decorative Serging Techniques

In past lessons you've mastered seams, edges, bindings, and trims. Now it's time to explore some of the special decorative techniques that make serger sewing so much fun. You can embellish fabric with flatlocking, trims, beading, and couching. You can gather, shirr, and fringe. You can even make a delicate, tatting-like lace with serger stitches.

Although decoratively serging seams and edges can ornament your latest fashion garments in high style, there are many more options available. By serging along folds, you can add embellishment anywhere on your fabric. Practically any decorative technique you see in ready-to-wear can be duplicated.

The lessons in this chapter will lead you through some of our favorite serger applications. You'll be delighted with the number of additional ornamental serging possibilities they open up for you.

Lesson 23. Gathering and Shirring

We use several different methods of serge-gathering to create ruffles, attach full skirts to waistbands or bodices, and to ornament other serger projects. Although it is generally fast and easy, serge-gathering works best on projects that do not require the wider seam allowances used for couture tailoring or delicate fabrics.

The width of the serge-gathered seam allowance is limited by the width of the serged stitch. The weight or thickness of your fabric and the project itself help determine what method to use. With any serge-gathering, a single layer of fabric will gather more than multiple layers.

Tension gathering

For easy gathering of lightweight fabric, tighten the needle tension almost all the way. Use a long stitch, your widest width, and a balanced 3-thread stitch. If you are using two needles instead, tighten both needle tensions. Vary the amount of gathers by changing the stitch length. A longer stitch length will gather the fabric more.

For speedier tension gathering, instead of tightening the tension dials, press or pull on the needle thread(s) immediately above your serger's first thread guide(s). (Fig. 6-1) This instant finger tensioning returns to normal just by releasing the thread.

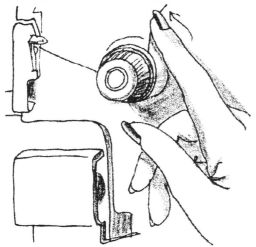

Fig. 6-1: *To quickly gather lightweight fabric, apply tension to needle thread.*

Differential-feed gathering

If your serger has differential feed, you can use it to easily gather lightweight fabrics. Use a wide, medium length, and balanced stitch. Adjust the differential feed to 2.0 for serge-gathering. To vary the amount of gathers, change the length of the stitch or the differential-feed setting.

To gather only one layer when you are serging two layers, lengthen your stitch to 4mm (or the longest possible). With the differential feed on 2.0, hold the top layer taut. On light-to medium-weight fabrics, the under layer will gather as you serge it to the top layer. Softer fabrics will gather more than stiff fabrics. Shorten your stitch length to reduce the amount of gathering.

Filler-cord gathering

To serge-gather medium- to heavy-weight fabrics, serge over a strand of filler thread such as buttonhole twist, crochet thread, or pearl cotton. (Fig. 6-2) Use a wide, medium to

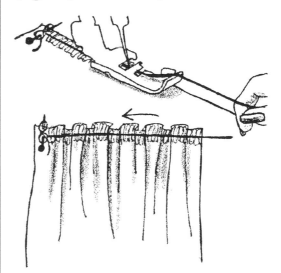

Fig. 6-2: *To gather medium- to heavy-weight fabric, serge over filler cord and pull to gather.*

short (2.5mm), and balanced 3-thread or 4-thread overedge stitch. Place the filler under the back and over the front of the presser foot, guiding it with the techniques from Lesson 4 (page 54). Serge over the filler, being careful not to cut it. Secure one end of the filler and pull the other end to gather the edge.

If your serger has a 4-thread overedge stitch, guide the filler between the two needles as you serge. (Fig. 6-3) The needle threads hold the filler in position for more controlled gathering.

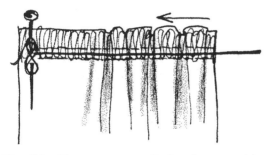

Fig. 6-3: *For more controlled gathering, place the filler thread between the two needles of a 4-thread overedge stitch.*

Thread-chain gathering

This technique uses thread chain as a gathering filler cord. Serge off a thread chain that is slightly longer than the edge to be gathered. Place the fabric under the presser foot, anchor one stitch in the fabric, and raise the needle. Without cutting the chain, pull it forward, over the top of the presser-foot front. Serge over the chain as if you were using filler thread, then draw it up to gather.

Serge-shirring

Parallel rows of serge-shirring can create a stretchy waistband or cuffs on your latest fashion garments. We prefer shirring the fabric first, before cutting it out. In addition to gathering in fabric lengthwise, the serge-shirred stitching takes up extra fabric width— about twice the width of the serged stitch for each row of shirring.

For easiest serge-shirring, begin with a long strip of elastic thread, cord, or clear elastic. Mark the desired length of your finished shirring on the elastic using a marking pen, leaving some extra at the beginning end. After serge-shirring over the elastic and fabric (see instructions below), secure the unmarked end of the elastic by pinning or sewing it and gather from the opposite end. (Fig. 6-4) Because you've serged over

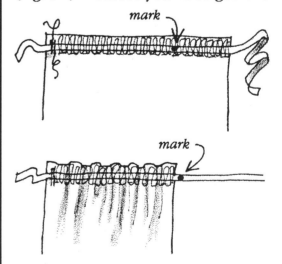

Fig. 6-4: *Shirr accurately by marking desired length on elastic. Serge over elastic, secure one end, and gather until mark is exposed.*

the elastic, not into it, it will pull easily. When the mark is exposed, secure and trim that end of the elastic and adjust the shirring evenly.

To serge-shirr using *elastic thread or cord*, adjust your serger for a short (2.5mm), narrow, and balanced 3-thread stitch. Place the thread under the back and over the front of the presser foot as for the filler-cord gathering. If your presser foot has an elastic/tape guide, place the elastic thread through the slots, too.

To begin, serge several stitches over the elastic until you reach the beginning mark you made. Fold the fabric right sides together and place it under the presser foot. Serge over the folded edge, being careful not to cut the fabric or the elastic. Secure one end of the elastic by pinning or sewing it and pull up the elastic to complete the shirring.

For more controlled shirring, serge over *elastic thread* using a 4-thread overedge stitch. Feed the elastic thread between the two needles, as for the filler cord, on page 112. The shirring will be a little bulkier, but will remain more uniformly distributed during wearing.

To serge-shirr with 1/8" *clear elastic*, adjust for a wide 3-thread stitch. Be careful to serge over, and not through, the elastic. Anchor and draw up the shirring as for the elastic thread, above.

An optional shirring method is to serge through a strip of wider clear elastic, stretching the elastic as you

serge. Use 1/4- to 3/8"-wide clear elastic. Adjust your serger for a medium stitch width and long stitch length. Thread the elastic under the back and over the front of the foot. Evenly section and mark the elastic and the fabric. Serge a few stitches on the elastic, then insert the folded fabric. Serge, stretching the elastic to match the section marks. (Fig. 6-5)

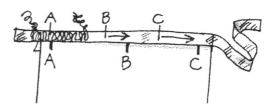

Fig. 6-5: Shirr while serging by stretching clear elastic to meet presectioned markings.

Project: Shirred Pony-Tail Tube

This simple yet pretty hair ornament is serge-shirred with elastic. Rolled-edge stitching adds a decorative finish. Vary the fabric and measurements to whip up tubes and headbands for any occasion. (Fig. 6-6)

Fig. 6-6: Shirred tubes dress up any hairstyle for special occasions or every day.

Stitch: 3-thread

Stitch length: Medium for elastic application; short (1.5 to 2mm) for rolled edge

Stitch width: Medium for elastic application; narrow for rolled edge

Thread: Matching or contrasting color

Needle: All-purpose or serger

Upper looper: All-purpose or serger for elastic application; decorative for rolled edge

Lower looper: All-purpose or serger

Tension: Balanced for elastic application; rolled edge for finishing

Needle: Size 11/75

Fabric: One strip 3-1/2" wide by 18" long

Notions: 24" of elastic cord or 1-1/3 yards of elastic thread (used double-strand)

1. Allowing a 2" tail, thread the elastic cord (or two strands of elastic thread) under the back and over the front of the presser foot. Serge several stitches over the elastic with a medium-width, balanced stitch.

2. Fold the fabric strip right sides together. Serge over the elastic on the folded fabric edge, being careful not to cut or sew through the elastic.

3. Secure one end of the elastic. Pull the opposite end to gather the fabric (to about 6" to 7" finished).

4. With the fabric ends flat and with the right sides of both ends together, straight-stitch the ends into a tube,

back-stitching over the elastic to secure. (Fig. 6-7) Knot the elastic ends and trim.

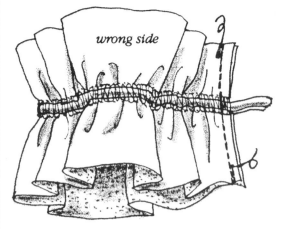

Fig. 6-7: *After pulling elastic to gather, straight-stitch to form tube. Backstitch over elastic to secure.*

5. Fold the fabric wrong sides together. Finish the tube by serge-seaming with a rolled edge, overlapping the beginning stitching to finish.

Lesson 24. Serger Lace

One of our favorite details for finishing dainty tucks on garment fronts and collars, serger lace also has interesting applications on numerous craft and accessory projects.

This lace is made by merely overlapping rows of balanced 3-thread serging. The appearance of serger lace can be varied by the thread used in the loopers and the number of rows of serging (more rows create a wider lace). Using buttonhole twist will give the look of a hand-crocheted edge. Lightweight thread creates a more delicate effect.

1. Adjust your serger for a wide, long, and balanced 3-thread stitch.

2. Serge one row of stitching to the fabric, allowing all but the needleline to hang off the edge. Leave at least a 4" thread chain at each end.

3. Overlap a second row of serging with the needle inside the overlocking loops of the first row of stitching. (Fig. 6-8)

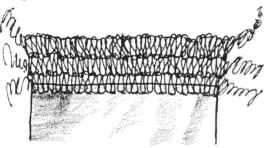

Fig. 6-8: *Overlap rows of 3-thread serging to form lace.*

4. To make wider lace, continue overlapping rows of serging to the width desired. It may take a little practice to position the needle just inside the loops. If the needle misses stitching inside the loops, you will have a hole in the lace. In this case, simply find the shortest thread (the needle thread) and pull it. The loops will fall away from the previous stitching, and you may serge the row again.

5. If you want to ruffle the lace, gently stretch it parallel to the edge. (Fig. 6-9)

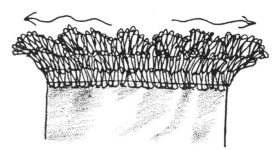

Fig. 6-9: *Gently stretch lace to ruffle.*

Serger lace tucks

Serger lace tucks are easier if you serge onto the fabric before cutting out the project. Begin by folding the fabric on the first tuck line. Serge-finish the edge with the needle about 1/8" inside the fold. Allow the loops to hang off the edge of the fabric. (Use a blindhem foot or ornamental stitching guide to ensure even stitching.) Continue folding and serging the tucks, using the presser foot to guide your stitching evenly. (Fig. 6-10) For wider lace tucks, serge another row of stitching inside the first row of loops. More delicate care may be required for this wider lace.

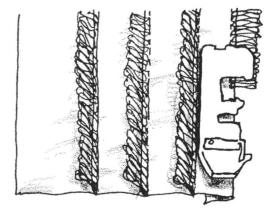

Fig. 6-10: *Serge even lace tucks by guiding presser-foot edge along previous row.*

Lacy fishline ruffles

To add a lace finish on the edge of fishline ruffles, apply the fishline according to the instructions in Lesson 8 (page 66). Serge the first row of lace with the needle just inside the rolled edge. Serge additional rows for wider lace.

Lace-trimmed wires

Serger lace also can be used to trim fine, flexible wires for craft projects. Cover the wire with a narrow rolled-edge stitch, guiding the wire under the back and over the front of the presser foot, **serging slowly**.

Adjust your serger for a wide, long, and balanced 3-thread stitch. Serge over the covered wire, keeping it between the needle and the knife, with the stitch loops hanging off the edge. Serge additional rows to make wider lace. Shape the lace-trimmed wire as desired and twist the ends together. (Fig. 6-11) Secure all the thread ends with seam sealant.

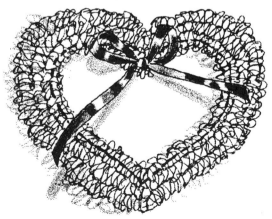

Fig. 6-11: *Serge lace over covered wire and shape as desired.*

Project: Serger-Lace Flower

A delicate flower is made by adding rows of serger lace to a strip of bias tricot. After serge-gathering, apply stiffening agent to the flower to keep it fresh and fluffy. Vary the size of the flower or the type of thread used. Attach your finished sample to the padded picture frame completed in Lesson 18 (page 94). (Fig. 6-12)

Fig. 6-12: *Make a delicate flower by gathering serger lace.*

Stitch: 3-thread
Stitch length: Long
Stitch width: Widest
Thread:
    Needle: All-purpose or serger
    Upper looper: All-purpose or serger
    Lower looper: All-purpose or serger

Tension: Balanced
Needle: Size 11/75
Notions: 18" of 5/8"-wide *Seams Great* or other bias tricot; stiffening spray or dip, such as *Stiffy* or *TAC Spray Stiff*

1. Apply serger lace to one long edge of the bias tricot. Begin with one row of stitching on the tricot, then add four more rows of stitching to complete the lace. (Fig. 6-13)

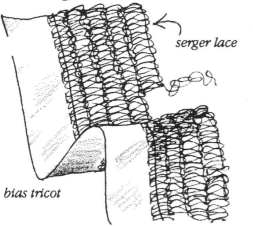

serger lace

bias tricot

Fig. 6-13: Serge four rows of lace on edge of 18" tricot strip.

2. Serge-gather the unfinished side of the tricot using the tension or differential feed methods in Lesson 23 (page 111). If the edge does not gather tightly, pull the needle thread (the shortest thread) to gather it further.

3. Spray (or dip) the flower with stiffening solution, following the directions on the bottle.

4. Glue or hand-tack the finished flower to the padded picture frame, covering the joined ends of the piped binding.

Lesson 25. Decorative Flatlocking

In Lesson 3, we discussed basic flatlocking as it relates to flatlocked seams. Flatlocking also can be applied on folds, so it can be used as decorative detailing anywhere on a garment or project. Among its varied applications, we've seen flatlocking stitched at angles across the front of an embellished sweatshirt or added as a delicate accent on dressier cuffs and collars.

In the following techniques, unless otherwise specified, it is assumed that your serger is adjusted to basic flatlocking tensions and that you will use either 2- or 3-thread flatlocking. See page 47 for details. Loosen the needle tension enough to allow the serging to pull flat after being stitched. For 3-thread flatlocking tighten the lower looper until it forms a straight line.

For most flatlocking, it is not necessary to disengage the upper knife. Simply move the fabric fold to the left of the knife about half of the stitch width. This also allows the stitches to hang off the edge for the flattest flatlocking. Use a blindhem foot (or ornamental stitching guide) to stitch evenly.

In addition to balanced 3-thread flatlocking, other novelty flatlocking effects can be achieved by changing tensions, stitch widths, and thread types.

Corded flatlocking

Flatlocking does not always require a wide stitch width. Narrow, satin-stitch flatlocking gives the appearance of cording or piping. For a more corded effect, tighten the needle tension slightly to raise the stitch. (Fig. 6-14) Shorten the stitch length for maximum thread coverage. A narrow ladder stitch will show from the underside.

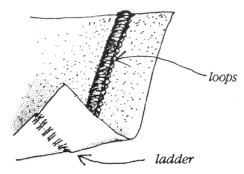

Fig. 6-14: For corded flatlocking, tighten needle tension.

Safety-stitch flatlocking

Flatlock with a wide 4-thread overedge stitch for safety-stitch flatlocking. Use a short- to medium-length, wide stitch and loosen both needle threads. (Fig. 6-15) On the underside, the ladder stitch will look identical to a 2- or 3-thread flatlock. The loops on the top side will have an extra right needle-thread line showing.

Safety-stitch flatlocking may not pull completely flat if you are unable to loosen your needle tensions enough. An option for this stitch is to create a raised fold underneath the flatlocked loops using a slightly tighter needle tension. (Fig. 6-15)

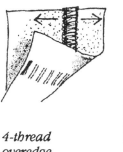

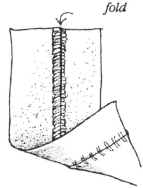

4-thread overedge stitch

Fig. 6-15: Loosen both needle tensions for safety-stitch flatlocking. With slightly tighter tension, a fold forms underneath loops.

Balanced flatlocking

Basic 3-thread flatlocking can be adjusted so the looper tensions are balanced, with the upper and lower looper stitches overlocking in the center of the stitch. (Fig. 6-16) The needle tension remains loose so the stitch will lie flat. Use contrasting thread colors in the loopers for a multicolored stitch.

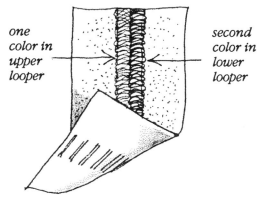

one color in upper looper

second color in lower looper

Fig. 6-16: Flatlocking with balanced looper tensions creates two-toned stitch.

Mock hemstitching

For mock hemstitching, simply straight-stitch through a wide flatlocked stitch. For the ladder side out, flatlock with the right sides together. Pull the fabric flat. Top-stitch from the wrong side with monofilament nylon thread in the bobbin and thread that matches the fabric in the needle. (Fig. 6-17) The ladder stitches will automatically bunch together. With this stitch, the serger needle thread is the ladder thread that shows, so any decorative thread used must be able to be threaded through the needle. Experiment with the stitch length for different effects.

Mock hemstitching also can be

 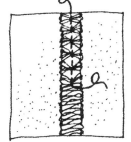

ladder on right side   *loops on right side*

Fig. 6-17: *Straight-stitch either the looped or ladder side of flatlocking to create mock hemstitching.*

flatlocked with the looped side out. (Fig. 6-17) Use the decorative thread in the looper. Flatlock and then top-stitch from the ladder side with monofilament nylon thread in the bobbin and thread that matches the fabric in the needle.

Serge-fagoting

Fagoting is a decorative flatlock stitch used for fabric embellishment or seams when the area will not be subjected to much stress, such as the fronts of blouses. Most often used in heirloom sewing on fine fabrics, fagoting is serged with the ladder side out. Use decorative thread in the needle. For inconspicuous loops (they may be seen from the top side after the edges are pulled apart), use monofilament nylon thread in the upper looper.

If you apply serge-fagoting to your garment fabric before cutting it out, establish a fagoting seamline and cut along it. Serge-finish the seam allowances and press them to the wrong side. Adjust for a long, wide flatlock stitch. With right sides together and the folds aligned, flatlock with the needle barely catching the edge of the fabric. Pull the stitching flat and press carefully. (Fig. 6-18)

Fig. 6-18: *For serge-fagoting, press seam allowances back. Flatlock, barely catching folds. Then pull stitches flat.*

For further embellishment, thread 1/8"-wide ribbon through the ladder stitches. Securely top-stitch the seam allowances on both sides of the fagoting, using a decorative stitch on your sewing machine.

Now center your pattern over the yardage and cut out.

Project: Sampler Pin Cushion

Practice these new techniques by making rows of decorative flatlocking on this handy pin cushion. Select a soft, woven fabric and tone-on-tone thread for a subtle effect. (Fig. 6-19)

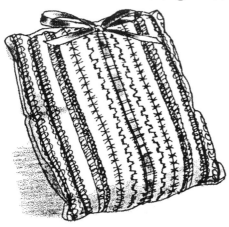

Fig. 6-19: Display decorative flatlocking options on a pretty pin cushion.

Stitch: 2- or 3-thread and 4-thread overedge
Stitch length: Short (1 to 2mm) for corded flatlocking, balanced flatlocking, and mock hemstitching; medium for safety-stitch; and long for fagoting
Stitch width: Narrow for corded; widest for all others

Thread: Same tone as fabric; monofilament nylon for bobbin
Needle(s): All-purpose, serger, or rayon
Upper looper: All-purpose, serger, or rayon
Lower looper: All-purpose or serger; contrasting color for balanced; rayon for 2-thread
Tension: Flatlock, unless otherwise indicated
Needle(s): Size 11/75
Fabric: 1/4 yard batiste, organdy, or broadcloth
Notions: 1/3 yard of 1/8"-wide satin ribbon—same tone as fabric and thread; polyester fiberfill for stuffing

1. Cut one 9" square from the fabric. Cut the square in half on the lengthwise grain.

2. On one long side of each piece, press 1/2" to the wrong side. With right sides together, apply fagoting. Pull the piece flat and weave the ribbon through the fagoted stitch. Decoratively top-stitch on both sides of the fagoting.

3. On both sides of the fagoting, with right sides together, serge a row of mock hemstitching a presser foot's width away from the fagoting. Topstitch from the wrong side with monofilament nylon in the bobbin.

4. Serge a row of balanced flatlocking on either side of the mock hemstitching, using a contrasting tone of thread in the lower looper. Use the presser-foot width as a stitching guide.

5. On either side of the balanced flatlocking, serge a row of narrow corded flatlocking. Then, if your serger has a 4-thread overedge stitch, add rows of safety-stitch flatlocking.

6. Cut one 6" by 7" rectangle from the flatlocked fabric and two 6" by 7" rectangles from the unfinished fabric.

7. Using one of the plain rectangles as a backing for the flatlocked piece, place the right sides of the rectangles together. Serge-seam with a wide, medium length, and balanced 3-thread or 4-thread overedge stitch. Leave an opening on one side to stuff the fiberfill.

8. Stuff the pin cushion and hand-tack the opening closed.

Lesson 26. Fringing

We see fringing on everything from scarves and garment edges to table-cloths and napkins. Using either flatlocking or balanced stitching, you can add a stable, decorative accent to the edge of any fringe. For fastest fringing, choose a fabric that ravels easily.

Flatlocked fringe

Choose balanced flatlocking or one of the other flatlocking options in Lesson 25 (page 117).

1. Select the width of fringe desired and pull a thread to mark the lines—at least 1" from the edge.

2. Fold your fabric wrong sides together and flatlock over the fringe line with a short- to medium-length, medium-width stitch. Use a matching or contrasting thread color in both the upper looper and the needle.

3. Start at a corner where the marked lines intersect. Flatlock to the next intersection and (before turning) pull the previous stitching flat. (Fig. 6-20) Fold the next side, turn the fabric a quarter turn, and repeat for the remaining sides.

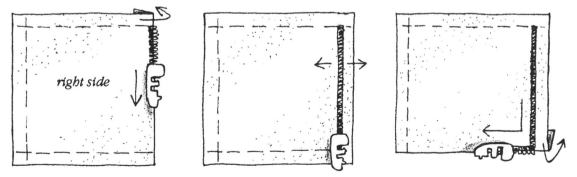

Fig. 6-20: For flatlocked fringe, serge on fold between intersecting lines. Pull stitching flat, turn square corner, and repeat for adjoining side.

4. Secure the ends by weaving the thread chains under the stitching.

5. For easiest fringing, clip from the cut edge to (but not through) the stitching every 2". Fringe to the stitching line by pulling out the horizontal threads.

Tucked fringe

For this edging option, serge a tuck and then top-stitch it down to the fabric next to the area to be fringed.

1. Put decorative thread in the upper looper and adjust for a short, medium to wide, and balanced 3-thread stitch.

2. Pull a thread 1-1/4" from the edges to mark the fringing lines.

3. Fold under 1-1/4" to the wrong side and, with the wrong side up, serge-finish along the fold to form a tuck. At the corner, serge to the intersection of the marked lines. Raise

the presser foot, pull the fabric back behind the needle, and serge off. (Fig. 6-21)

4. Fold the serge-finished tuck away from the cut edge. Fold the adjoining edge along the marked line, in the same manner as for step 3. Clear the stitches from your stitch finger and position the needle directly over the outside edge of the previous stitching. Begin by serging over the previous tuck, then continue serging the edge as in step 3.

5. Repeat steps 3 and 4 for the remaining edges to be fringed.

6. Press the finished tucks away from the edges. Hide the thread chains under the tucks and top-stitch to secure.

7. Clip the cut edges below the tucks every 2" and fringe by pulling out the horizontal threads.

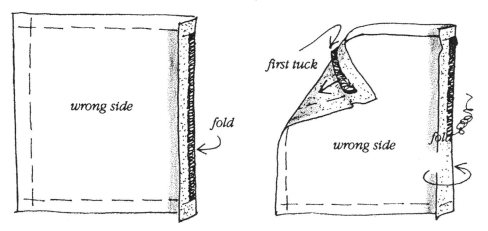

Fig. 6-21: *For tucked fringe, use a balanced stitch. Serge between intersecting marks and fold tuck toward center. Repeat for adjoining sides.*

Project: Fringed Triangle Scarf

This fashionable scarf is made from a folded square of challis. The double thickness gives a thick fringed edge, and the bias fold drapes softly at the neckline. Attach the corded frog closures made in Lesson 21 (page 107). Whether you wear the scarf with the frogs in front or at the shoulder, it will stay securely in place. (Fig. 6-22)

Fig. 6-22: *Fringe two sides of a folded challis triangle. Secure with frog closures from Lesson 21.*

Stitch: 3-thread
Stitch length: Medium (2.5mm to 3mm)
Stitch width: Medium to wide
Thread: Contrasting color
   Needle: All-purpose or serger
   Upper looper: Heavy rayon, such as *Decor 6* or pearl rayon
   Lower looper: All-purpose or serger
Tension: Balanced
Needle: Size 11/75
Fabric: 1 yard wool challis

1. Cut a 36" square of challis. On two adjoining sides, pull a thread or press-mark the fabric 1-1/4" from each side to mark the fringe lines.

2. Fold the scarf in half diagonally with the two marked fringe lines on top.

3. On one side, fold both layers of the fringe allowance 1-1/4" to the back side, along the marked line. Lightly press. Then turn the back side up and serge-finish the fold, stopping at the point where the two marked lines intersect (Fig. 6-23). Raise the presser foot, pull the remaining fabric behind the needle, and chain off.

4. Press the serged tuck toward the fabric, wrapping the thread chains underneath. Top-stitch to secure.

5. Repeat steps 3 and 4 for the other fringed side. Begin serge-finishing with the needle positioned exactly on the outer edge of the previous stitching at the point of the scarf. Serge to the end of the fabric and chain off.

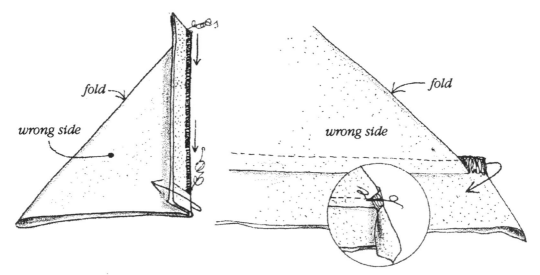

Fig. 6-23: *The fringe and tuck will extend past the folded edge of the scarf. Fold end under and top-stitch.*

6. On the two scarf points adjoining the folded edge, the fringe allowance and serged tuck will extend past the edge of the scarf. Fold the extension back and, to secure it, top-stitch across the tuck stitching. (Fig. 6-23) Clip the fringe allowance every 2" and pull out the horizontal threads.

7. Hand-tack the frog closures made in Lesson 21 (page 107) to the unfringed scarf edges. Position them 8" and 11" from the bottom of the fringe. Attach the frogs so the edges of the scarf meet, but don't overlap, under the frogs.

Lesson 27. Serging over Trim

If a decorative thread, yarn, or ribbon is too bulky (or not flexible enough) to thread through your loopers, you have the option of serging over it. In order to fully cover a trim with serging, it must be narrow enough to fit between the needle and the knives. The upper looper also must be able to clear the trim without catching so the stitches will form evenly.

To serge over decorative trim, adjust the stitch width so that it is wide enough to cover the trim. The length of the stitch will depend on how much of the trim you want to expose. Start with a medium stitch length for testing. Use a balanced 3-thread stitch or a 2- or 3-thread flatlock. Use monofilament nylon or matching serger thread in the upper looper to emphasize the trim.

Place the trim under the back and over the front of the presser foot, guiding it between the needle and the knives. Use the same techniques for serging over filler cord in Lesson 4 (page 54). Allow several inches of trim to extend behind the foot.

For easier feeding, begin serging over the trim for several stitches with no fabric underneath. Then insert the fabric under the trim and serge slowly. Be careful not to stitch through the trim or cut it with the knives. Especially if it's bulky, you may need to hold the trim taut to guide it out from under the back of the presser foot.

Flatlocking over ribbon

Try flatlocking over a ribbon to cover a seam. The ribbon should be narrow enough to be serged over without cutting or stitching through it. The 1/8"-wide ribbon works with most wide stitch widths. A 1/16"-wide ribbon is also available for a narrower 3-thread stitch.

1. Serge-seam the fabric with right sides together.

2. Place the ribbon under the back and over the front of the presser foot, between the needle and the knives. Adjust for a flatlock and serge a few stitches over the ribbon.

3. Fold the fabric on the seamline, wrong sides together. Raise the presser foot and put the fabric halfway under the ribbon. Flatlock through all layers, with the stitches just covering the ribbon edges. (Fig. 6-24)

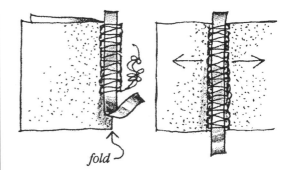

Fig. 6-24: Center ribbon along fold of fabric before flatlocking. Pull flat.

4. Pull the stitching flat and the ribbon will cover the seamline.

Flatlocking over lace and ribbon

Another decorative technique is to center a layer of double-edged lace over the seamline on the right side of the fabric. Then fold the lace and the fabric along the seamline and flatlock the ribbon on top (through all layers) using the method above for flatlocking over ribbon. (Fig. 6-25)

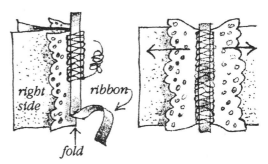

Fig. 6-25: Flatlock to attach a layer of ribbon and lace to fabric.

Flatlocking over yarn

Flatlocking over yarn with monofilament nylon thread appears to leave the yarn floating on the fabric surface.

1. Fold the fabric right sides together with the yarn inside the fold. (Fig. 6-26)

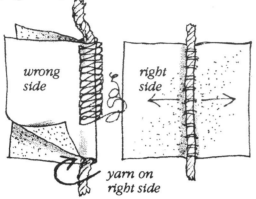

wrong side

right side

yarn on right side

Fig. 6-26: Flatlock over decorative yarn from wrong side. Only the ladder stitch shows on right side.

2. Thread monofilament nylon in the needle and matching all-purpose or serger thread in the looper(s).

3. Serge the fold with a wide, long flatlock stitch.

4. Pull the fold flat. From the right side, the yarn floats on the surface, held invisibly by the monofilament.

S **Special Tip:** If you have difficulty catching the yarn in the fold, baste it with a zigzag stitch to hold it in place for the flatlocking. Use monofilament nylon thread in the needle for invisible zigzag basting.

Project: Heart-shaped Jewelry Holder

This feminine jewelry holder is decoratively finished by flatlocking over ribbon. Covered hooks hold necklaces tangle-free. (Fig. 6-27)

Fig. 6-27: Pillowed jewelry holder keeps bracelets and necklaces tangle-free.

Stitch: 2- or 3-thread for flatlocking; 3-thread or 4-thread overedge for serge-seaming
Stitch length: Medium to long for flatlocking; medium for serge-seaming
Stitch width: Widest
Thread: Matching color
   Needle(s): All-purpose or serger
   Upper looper: Monofilament nylon for flatlocking; all-purpose or serger for serge-seaming
   Lower looper: All-purpose or serger; monofilament nylon for 2-thread flatlocking

Tension: Flatlocking for ribbon
   application; balanced for serge-
   seaming
Needle(s): Size 11/75
Fabric: 1/4 yard batiste; 1/4 yard
   lace yardage (will make two
   holders)
Notions: 2 yards 1/8"-wide satin
   ribbon (1/16"-wide for narrower
   stitch widths); 5 large covered
   hooks (used on heavy coats); one
   yard 3/4"-wide ruffled lace;
   fiberfill for stuffing

1. Using the pattern grid (Fig. 6-28),
cut one lace and two fabric heart
pieces.

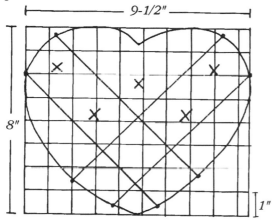

*Fig. 6-28: Jewelry holder pattern, with ribbon
and hook placement marked.*

2. With wrong sides of the lace
together, flatlock four strips of ribbon
to the lace heart piece, as shown on
the pattern grid.

3. Adjust the serger for a balanced
stitch. Layer one fabric heart under

the lace heart. Fold 1/2" of the ruffled
lace to the wrong side. Beginning at
the lower point, place the right side of
the ruffled lace against the right side
of the two heart layers (lace heart on
top). Serge the lace to the heart,
pulling the edge out straight at the
inside corner on the top of the heart.
Overlap the beginning lace at the
point.

4. With the ruffled lace sandwiched
between, place the remaining fabric
heart right sides together with the lace
heart. Beginning at the lower point,
serge-seam, leaving a 3" opening for
the stuffing.

5. Turn the heart right side out and
stuff with fiberfill. Hand-tack the
opening closed.

6. Hand-tack a bow and hanging
loop at the top and five hooks on the
front, as in the finished view above.

Lesson 28.
Sequin, Bead, and
Pearl Application

Strands of colorful beads, elegant
pearls, and shiny sequins can be
serged to edges or anywhere else on
your garment or project. Use them for
bridalwear, holiday glitz, or just for
fun.

Applying beads and pearls

Beaded trims (available at craft and
fabric stores or through mail order)
can be applied with a balanced, rolled

edge or flatlock stitch. The beads must be small enough to fit between the needle and knives and for the upper looper to pass over them. Purchase enough yardage for thorough testing before application.

Adjust for a stitch slightly longer and wider than the beads you are applying. Use monofilament nylon thread in the upper looper and matching all-purpose or serger thread in the needle and lower looper. Both a 2-thread flatlock and 2-thread rolled edge work well for the application of bead trim, because less thread coverage provides a neater finish.

To apply bead trim, place it under the back and over the front of the presser foot, as if serging over any filler. Allow 2-3" to extend beyond the back of the presser foot. If your foot does not have a channel in the back for the beading to feed through, you will need to remove the presser foot and carefully guide the trim manually. (Fig. 6-29) Slowly serge

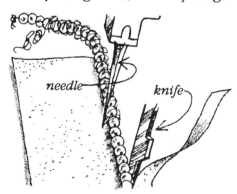

Fig. 6-29: Serge over beaded trim placed between the needle and the knife.

over several inches of the beading before inserting the fabric. If you are flatlocking, remember to allow the stitches to hang off the edge.

To serge off, cut the trim and carefully serge over the trim end. If necessary, use seam sealant to secure the beads before cutting.

Beaded piping

To make a piping strip of beads or pearls, serge the strands to a folded 1-1/4"-wide bias strip of tricot or other lightweight fabric.

Applying sequins

To serge over sequin trim, the sequins must be narrow enough for the looper thread to lock over them. Place the trim so that the sequins overlap away from the presser foot. (Fig. 6-30) Disengage the knife and serge over the sequin trim with a long stitch length. Use monofilament

Fig. 6-30: Overlap sequin trim away from presser foot.

nylon thread or matching thread in the upper looper. After serging, slide the upper looper threads between the sequins so no thread is visible.

Project: Bead-edged Flower

A strand of pearl beading can be applied to a folded edge of organza to create an elegant flower accessory. Attach it to a pin or hair comb, or use it to adorn the evening bag you'll make in Lesson 36, page 156. (Fig. 6-31)

Fig. 6-31: *Beaded trim dresses up the edges of a flower.*

Stitch: 2- or 3-thread for bead application; 3-thread for serge-gathering
Stitch length: Medium—slightly longer than the individual bead
Stitch width: Narrow—to cover the bead; widest for serge-gathering
Thread: Matching color
    Needle: All-purpose or serger
    Upper looper: Monofilament nylon, all-purpose, or serger
    Lower looper: All-purpose or serger; monofilament nylon for 2-thread rolled edge
Tension: Rolled edge for bead application; balanced for serge-gathering

Needle: Size 11/75
Fabric: 5" of organza or georgette (45" wide)
Notions: 1-1/2 yards of pearl beading

1. Fold the fabric strip in half lengthwise. Serge the pearl beading to the folded edge with a rolled-edge stitch.

2. Adjust your serger for serge-gathering, using one of the techniques in Lesson 23 (page 110). With the presser foot raised, begin the gathering by carefully serging over the pearls at one end. Lower the presser foot and taper to the cut edges, finishing the edges. (Fig. 6-32) Taper off at the other end, raising the presser foot as you serge over the pearls.

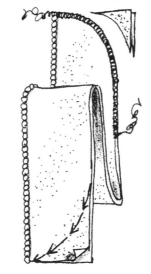

Fig. 6-32: *Taper strip ends while serge-gathering. Raise foot when serging over the pearls.*

3. If you want more gathering, pull on the needle thread (the shortest thread in the chain). Shape the strip into a flower and hand-tack the gathered edges together.

Lesson 29. Serge-Couching

Couching braid (for embellishing fabric with curved or looped designs) can be created on your serger. Create the braid by serging over a filler, such as strands of heavier thread or cord, with a rolled-edge stitch. Or make the puffed serged braid featured in Lesson 21 (page 105) by serging over tubes of bias fabric or thick yarn.

Use heavier decorative thread in the upper looper and matching all-purpose or serger thread in the needle and lower looper. Thread the filler under the back and over the front of the presser foot using the techniques in Lesson 4 (page 54).

For a flatter couching braid, use a lighter-weight filler or fewer filler threads. Or if you use heavy thread in the upper looper, you may choose not

to have a filler at all. Adjust your serger for a short, narrow, and balanced 2- or 3-thread stitch. Tighten the lower looper slightly. The lower looper thread should not show, and any filler should be covered entirely by the upper looper thread.

Sew couching braid to your fabric by straight-stitching through it, zigzagging over it, or stitching beside it with a blindhem stitch. Straight-stitching works best on flatter braid. You may need to zigzag over a thicker braid. (Fig. 6-33) Use monofilament nylon or matching thread in the needle. For easier couching application, use a

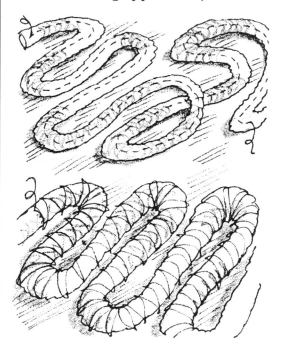

Fig. 6-33: *Straight-stitch flatter couching braid, zigzag over thicker braid.*

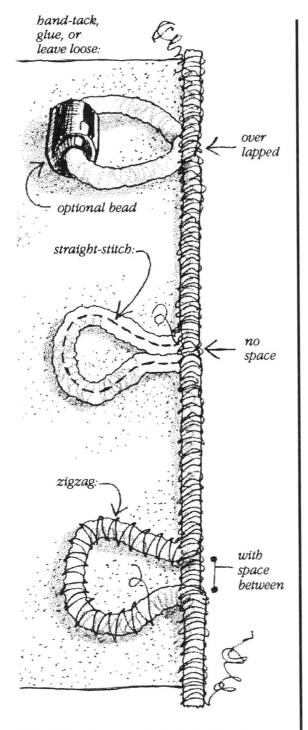

*hand-tack,
glue, or
leave loose:*

over lapped

optional bead

straight-stitch:

no space

zigzag:

with space between

fusible thread in the lower looper when making the braid. Loosen the lower looper tension to allow more coverage for the fusible thread. Fuse the braid to your fabric to complete the couching. Or for more durability after fusing, zigzag over the braid.

To apply couching directly with your serger, use a balanced or flatlock stitch. This application requires straighter design lines, but loops can be formed in the couching braid to add interest. The loops are later glued, hand-tacked, straight-stitched, or zigzagged down. (Fig. 6-34) Or you may choose to thread a bead on the loop as you work, before securing the second side.

Fig. 6-34: *Serge-couch straight edge, leaving loops. Variations add interest.*

Project: Couched Tree Ornament

Little couched pillows add a festive touch to any Christmas tree. They're made quickly with rolled-edge finishing and serged couching braid. Vary the fabric, thread color, and couching design to individualize each ornament. (Fig. 6-35)

Fig. 6-35: *Couching personalizes an easy Christmas ornament.*

Stitch: 2- or 3-thread
Stitch length: Short (1mm to 2mm)
Stitch width: Narrow
Thread: Contrasting color
  Needle: Matching for 3-thread braid and rolled edge; fusible for 2-thread braid; woolly or monofilament nylon for 2-thread rolled edge
  Upper looper: Woolly nylon (3-thread only)
  Lower looper: Fusible for 3-thread braid; woolly nylon for 2-thread braid; woolly or monofilament nylon for 3-thread rolled edge
Tension: Balanced for braid; rolled edge for serge-finishing
Needle: Size 11/75 (14/90 if using fusible thread)
Fabric: 1/6 yard woven fabric
Notions: Heavy filler thread (crochet or pearl cotton); fiberfill for stuffing

1. Cut two 4" fabric squares on the bias grain.

2. With a vanishing marker, draw a couching design on both squares. Use initials or simple designs such as bells, stars, or Christmas trees. (Use cookie cutters for design sources.)

3. With a narrow, balanced stitch and your serger threaded according to the specifications above, serge over four strands of filler to create one yard of braid.

4. Fuse the braid over the designs on the squares, tucking the ends underneath. Zigzag over the braid with monofilament nylon thread.

5. Adjust your serger for a rolled edge and serge over two strands of the filler, making a 6" chain.

6. Place the two squares wrong sides together, making certain the designs are going in the same direction.

7. Serge-finish three edges with a rolled edge. Stuff the pillow and complete by serge-finishing the final edge.

8. Form a hanging loop from the filler chain (step 5) and hand-tack it to the upper corner of the ornament.

7. Decorative Serged Closures

■ **Lesson 30. Lapped and Top-stitched Zippers**
■ **Lesson 31. Zipped Double-bound Edges**
■ **Lesson 32. Serge-picked Zippers**
■ **Lesson 33. Serge-bound Buttonholes**
■ **Lesson 34. Serged Elastic Button Loops**

Although we have steered away from construction techniques in this book, this chapter is an exception. Decorative closures can be an important design element in your serging projects. For example, a colorful top-stitched zipper down the front of a top or pretty serge-bound buttonholes to match your jacket's edge-finishing provide an outstanding ornamental feature on your garment. Before discussing decorative closures, we will first outline the techniques for applying them. None are very complicated, and a few are actually simple.

Lesson 30. Lapped and Top-stitched Zippers

Zippers can be applied to garments and craft projects using several methods. The simplest application involves serge-finishing both fabric edges with a narrow decorative finish and top-stitching them single-layer to the right side of the zipper tape. This sporty technique leaves the zipper teeth exposed. Colorful zippers and a variety of thread choices lend a wide range of combinations.

Experiment with different edge finishes discussed in Chapter 4. Adjust for a short satin-stitch length for best thread coverage. Test first, though, because too short a stitch can cause an edge to stretch out.

For more durable edges, especially on lightweight or knit fabrics, press under the seam allowance and serge-finish on the fold. Add 1/2" allowances if there are none, press them under, and serge-finish.

Follow these simple steps for a lapped and top-stitched zipper:

1. With decorative thread in the upper looper, serge-finish the edges to be zipped. Serge from the right side, directly on the seamlines or over the fold.

2. Place the serge-finished edges on the top side of the zipper tape, next to the teeth.

3. Top-stitch with a straight-stitch along the needleline of the serging. (Fig. 7-1)

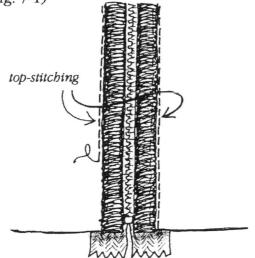

top-stitching

Fig. 7-1: *Top-stitch lapped zipper next to needleline of decorative serging.*

The lapped and top-stitched zipper application is most often used when both ends of the zipper will be crossed and anchored by an intersecting seam.

Project: Serged Pencil Case

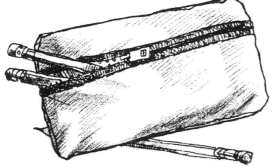

Fig. 7-2: *Pencil case features a colorful lapped and top-stitched zipper.*

This zippered pencil case is a quick and easy project for your favorite student. Select fabrics and decorative edging to suit any taste. (Fig. 7-2)

Stitch: 3-thread for decorative; 3-thread or 4-thread overedge for serge-seaming

Stitch length: Short for decorative; medium for serge-seaming

Stitch width: Narrow to medium for decorative; wide for serge-seaming

Thread: Contrasting color for decorative; matching color for serge-seaming

Needle(s): All-purpose or serger

Upper looper: Cotton crochet for decorative; all-purpose or serger for serge-seaming

Lower looper: All-purpose or serger

Tension: Balanced

Needle(s): Size 14/90

Fabric: 1/6 yard denim (make two cases from 45"-wide fabric)

Notions: One 9" zipper in contrasting color

1. Cut two 10" by 5" rectangles from the denim. Cut one rectangle lengthwise into two pieces, one 10" by 1-1/2" and the other 10" by 3-1/2".

2. Adjust your serger for decorative edging. Serge-finish one long edge of each of the narrower rectangles, trimming slightly.

3. Bartack the zipper tape together next to the upper zipper stop with a short zigzag stitch.

4. Center one decorative edge over the right side of the zipper tape. Top-stitch over the needleline of the decorative stitching. Repeat for the other side.

5. Open the zipper and place the two rectangles wrong sides together. The zippered half will be slightly wider than the plain half. Serge-seam all four sides, trimming off the extra fabric. When serging over both ends of the zipper, serge slowly and guide your needle right next to the zipper stops. Turn the case right side out through the zipper opening.

Lesson 31. Zipped Double-bound Edge

This decorative lapped zipper application uses a wide double-bound edge to cover the zipper teeth. Like the lapped and top-stitched zipper, the zipped double-bound edge is most often used when both zipper ends will later be intersected by a seam. The zipper pull and teeth will be neatly hidden.

To use this application method with a wide 7.5mm stitch, cut any edge that will be double-bound 3/4" wider than your pattern. The extra allowance is necessary for the edge-finishing technique. For a narrower 5mm stitch, add 1/2" to 5/8" for the bound edge.

1. Place the zipper face down on the right side of the seamline, matching the zipper tape to the cut edge.

2. Adjust the serger for a narrow, medium-length stitch. Serge the zipper to the seam allowance, as shown. (Fig. 7-3) Do not trim the zipper tape. Hold the zipper and fabric taut to prevent the presser foot from slipping off the zipper teeth.

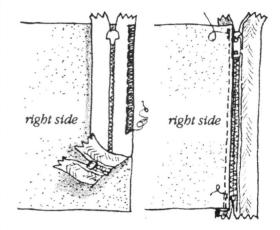

Fig. 7-3: Serge zipper to right side of fabric. Fold back allowance and top-stitch.

3. With the zipper right side up, form a fold in the seam allowance, close to the zipper teeth. Top-stitch the fold to the zipper tape.

4. Finish the fabric for the opposite side of the zipper with a double-bound edge (page 82).

5. Lap the double-bound edge over the zipper teeth and top-stitch in place. If your bound edge is a full 1/2" or more, you may choose to top-stitch on the center needleline. If the binding is narrower, top-stitch over the original top-stitching line.

Project: Dressed-up Cosmetic Bag

A wide double-bound edge hides the zipper on this quilted cosmetic bag. Show off your serging skills and please those on your gift list at the same time. (Fig. 7-4)

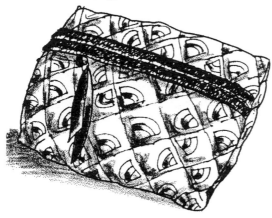

Fig. 7-4: *A double-bound edge hides the zipper on a quilted cosmetic bag.*

Stitch: 3-thread for decorative and zipper seaming; 3-thread or 4-thread overedge for serge-seaming

Stitch length: Short for decorative; medium for serge-seaming

Stitch width: Wide; narrow for zipper seaming

Thread: Contrasting color for decorative; matching color for serge-seaming

Needle(s): All-purpose or serger

Upper looper: Two colors of woolly nylon for decorative; all-purpose or serger for serge-seaming

Lower looper: All-purpose or serger for serge-seaming

Tension: Balanced

Needle(s): Size 11/75

Fabric: 1/3 yard quilted fabric (45"-wide fabric makes five bags)

Notions: One zipper 9" or longer; 6" of 1/4"-wide ribbon

1. Cut an 8" by 12" rectangle from the fabric.

2. Center the right side of the zipper on the right side of one short end of the fabric rectangle, matching the zipper tape to the cut edge. With a narrow stitch width, serge the zipper to the seam allowance.

3. On the other short end, press 3/4" to the wrong side. With decorative thread in the upper looper, serge-finish the fold from the wrong side. Carefully press the serged fold to the right side and top-stitch next to the overlocked loops. (See instructions for a double-bound edge, page 82.)

4. Fold the remaining fabric edge to the wrong side the same width as your previous decorative stitching. Serge over the fold with a contrasting thread color in the upper looper. Keep the needle right on the needleline of the previous stitching.

5. Lap the decorative edge over the unfinished side of the zipper so that the middle of the binding is next to the zipper teeth. With the zipper closed, top-stitch down the middle of the double-rolled edge (on top of the previous needle line), securing the decorative edge to the zipper tape. (Fig. 7-5)

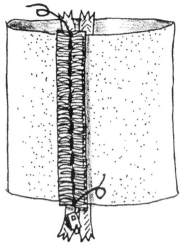

Fig. 7-5: Top-stitch decorative binding to right side of zipper tape.

6. Open the zipper and turn the bag inside out. Fold so the zipper is approximately 1-1/2" from the upper edge. Serge-seam the sides of the bag, slowly serging over the zipper tape. (Fig. 7-6)

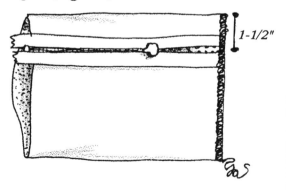

Fig. 7-6: Serge-seam bag sides from wrong side.

7. Turn the bag right side out. Knot the ribbon through the zipper pull.

Lesson 32. Serge-picked Zippers

This nifty (yet more complicated) zipper application produces results similar to a hand-picked zipper. Try both the centered and lapped methods in your fashion garments, from tailored to dressy. In addition to the decorative hand-picked look, the zipper is securely sewn to the seam allowance and all edges are neatly serge-finished. (Fig. 7-7)

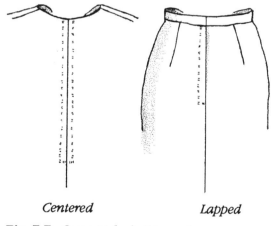

Centered   Lapped

Fig. 7-7: Serge-picked zippers give a decorative, hand-picked appearance.

For a serge-picked zipper, adjust your serger to its longest-length, balanced, 3-thread stitch. Follow the same procedures as when folding for a conventionally sewn blindhem. The needle of the serged stitch should barely catch the fold of the fabric.

Stitches will be visible from the right side, but with matching thread they will appear hand-picked. For accuracy, use a blindhem foot (or an ornamental stitching guide).

S **Special Tip:** We found that practicing the serged blindhem technique before applying the zipper is the key to a professionally applied serge-picked zipper.

Buy a zipper that is at least 1" longer than the garment opening. The excess zipper will be cut off at the top. For both application methods, machine baste the opening closed. Press the seam allowances open.

Centered application

1. Place the zipper face down on the basted seam with the teeth directly on the seamline. Machine baste the zipper to the seam allowance, as shown, ending at the lower zipper stop. (Fig. 7-8)

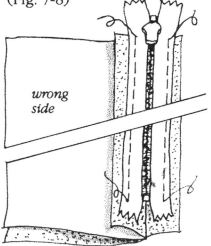

Fig. 7-8: Machine baste zipper to seam allowances.

2. Repeat step 1, basting the zipper to the other seam allowance.

3. With the wrong side of the zipper down, fold the fabric exactly 1/4" away from the seamline, as shown. (Fig. 7-9) Serge-pick the zipper, end-

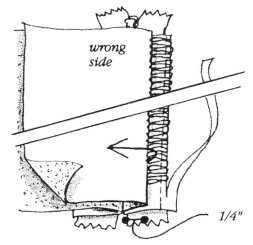

Fig. 7-9: Fold fabric back, leaving 1/4" between seam and foldline. Serge, barely catching needle in fold.

ing even with or above the lower zipper stop, making sure the seam allowance is folded exactly 1/4". Barely catch the needle in the fold of the fabric. The zipper tape and seam allowance will be trimmed slightly. Repeat for the other side of the zipper, starting even with or above the lower stop.

4. Pull the garment or project flat and press carefully.

5. To complete the bottom edge of the zipper, fold the fabric back from the lower edge of the zipper, as shown. (Fig. 7-10) With chalk or a

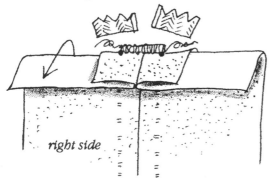

Fig. 7-10: *Fold fabric back at bottom of zipper. Trim zipper tape. Mark and serge-pick fabric between needlelines.*

marking pen, mark the needlelines on the fold, as shown. Trim the zipper tape to 1/4". Beginning and ending exactly on the markings, serge-pick the lower edge. Use seam sealant to secure the ends of the serging.

6. Pull the garment flat and press carefully. Remove the machine basting from the seamline.

Lapped application

1. Place the zipper face down on the basted seam with the teeth directly over the seamline.

2. Adjust the serger for a narrow, medium-length stitch. Serge the zipper to the seam allowance, beginning at the lower zipper stop. (Fig. 7-11) Do not trim the zipper tape. Hold the zipper and fabric taut to prevent the presser foot from slipping off the zipper teeth.

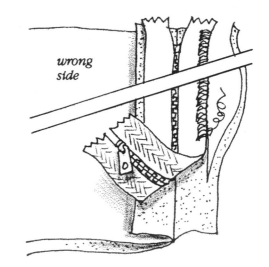

Fig. 7-11: *Center zipper over seamline. Beginning at lower zipper stop, serge zipper to right seam allowance.*

3. With the zipper right side up, form a fold in the seam allowance, close to the zipper teeth. Top-stitch the fold to the zipper tape, as shown. (Fig. 7-12)

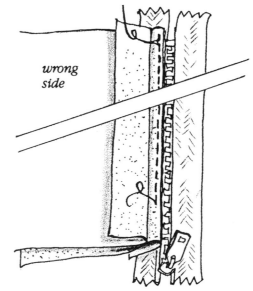

Fig. 7-12: *With zipper face up, fold seam allowance close to teeth. Top-stitch the fold.*

4. With the wrong side of the zipper down, machine baste the other side of the zipper tape to the seam allowance, beginning even with or above the lower zipper stop.

5. With the wrong side of the zipper still down, fold the fabric exactly 3/8" away from the seamline. (Fig. 7-13) Serge-pick one side as in step 3 of the centered application, beginning even with or above the lower zipper stop.

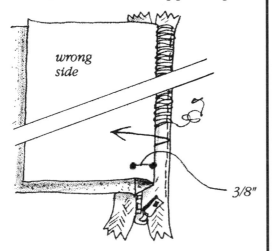

Fig. 7-13: Fold fabric back 3/8". Serge, barely catching needle in fold.

6. Fold the garment back at the bottom of the zipper. Mark, trim, serge-pick, and complete the application as in steps 5 and 6 of the centered method.

Project: Tailored Garment Bag

Although a serge-picked zipper is most often seen in our finest gar-

ments, it works equally well for other projects like this sophisticated garment bag. Everyone will think your tailor finished it by hand. (Fig. 7-14)

Fig. 7-14: Tailored garment bag with a centered serge-picked zipper.

Stitch: 3-thread for serge-picking; 3-thread or 4-thread overedge for serge-seaming
Stitch length: Longest for serge-picking; medium for serge-seaming
Stitch width: Wide (medium if using the blindhem foot)
Thread: Matching or contrasting color for serge-picking; matching for serge-seaming
Needle(s): All-purpose or serger
Upper looper: All-purpose or serger
Lower looper: All-purpose or serger

Tension: Balanced
Needle(s): Size 11/75
Fabric: 1-1/2 yard woven fabric—
    at least 54" wide
Notions: 42" zipper with one zipper
    pull (purchase from upholstery
    supply stores or by the yard from
    mail-order sources)

1. Make the pattern for the back of
the garment bag by tracing around a
plastic hanger at the top of the bag.
Extend the pattern 2" on both sides
and 50" in length. Add 1/2" seam
allowances to all sides, then curve out
the top for the hanger opening.
(Fig. 7-15)

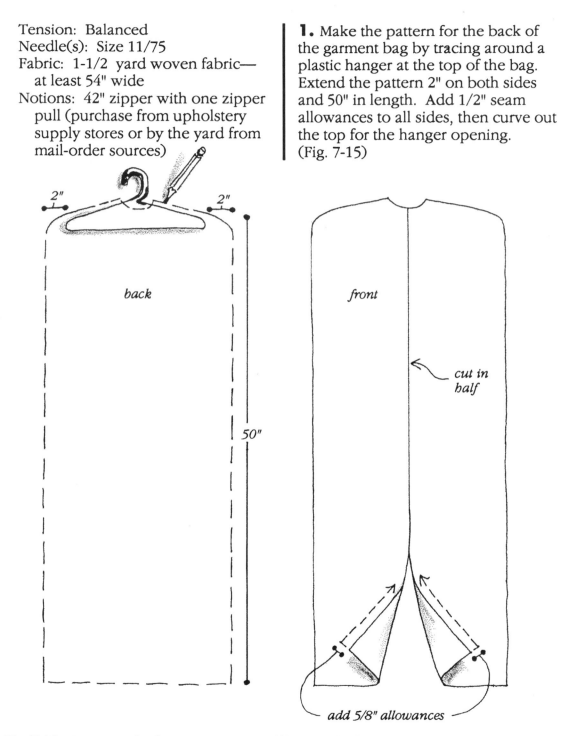

Fig. 7-15: *For pattern back, trace around top of hanger. Add 2" at each side and extend sides*
50". For front, trace back and add center seam allowances.

2. For the front pattern piece, trace the back and cut it in half lengthwise (for the center front opening). Add 5/8" seam allowances. (Fig. 7-15)

3. Cut out the back and the two front pieces.

4. Place the front pieces right sides together. Starting at the top of the bag, straight-stitch the seamline for 2". Back-stitch and lengthen your stitch for machine basting. Continue along the seamline, basting to within 8" of the bottom edge. Switch to a regular straight-stitch. Back-stitch and complete the seam.

5. Place the zipper pull on the upper edge of the zipper and bartack 1-1/2" from the top of the zipper tape, making sure the pull is below the bartack.

6. Place the zipper face down on the basted seam, with the teeth directly on the seamline and the top edge of the zipper tape 1/2" from the top edge of the bag. Starting at the top of the zipper tape, machine baste the center of the zipper tape to the seam allowance on each side, ending 1" from the bottom of the zipper.

7. With the wrong side of the zipper down, fold 1/4" away from the seamline on one side and serge-pick the zipper, barely catching the needle in the fold of the fabric. (Refer back to Fig. 7-9.)

 Note: If the knives do not trim the zipper tape smoothly, you will need to pretrim them before serge-picking. Repeat for the other side of the zipper.

8. Pull the bag flat and press carefully. Remove the basting threads.

9. Finish the lower part of the zipper by folding back the bag to the end of the zipper stitching. Trim the zipper to 1/4" and serge-pick between the two needlelines.

10. Serge-finish the top opening edge and the seam allowances below the zipper. Turn the top edge 1/4" to the wrong side and top-stitch to finish.

11. Open the zipper about 12". With right sides together, serge-seam the bottom edge of the bag. Then serge-seam both side seams of the bag. Weave the thread chains back through the serging. Turn the bag right side out through the zipper opening and tie a ribbon or cord to the zipper pull.

Lesson 33. Serge-bound Buttonholes

Buttonholes can be the bane of a sewing project, especially bound buttonholes with their complex and exacting procedure. But with your serger, decorative bound buttonholes are fast and easy. You can also use this technique for decorative welt pockets. Both can complement other decorative serging detail on your garment or project.

1. Accurately mark the buttonhole placements on the wrong side of the fabric and on the facing.

2. With pinking shears cut rectangles of lightweight nonwoven fusible interfacing for each buttonhole in the fabric and the facing. The rectangles should be 2" wide and 1" longer than the buttonholes. Place the rectangles, resin side up, over the buttonhole positions on the right side of the fabric and facing.

3. From the wrong side of the fabric, straight-stitch the buttonhole rectangle markings. (Fig. 7-16)

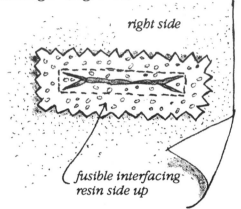

Fig. 7-16: *Straight-stitch buttonhole rectangles from wrong side, using markings as guide.*

4. Cut the buttonholes open, clipping to the corners. Carefully turn the interfacing through to the wrong side. Working with the long edges first, finger-press, then fuse, using the tip of your iron.

5. Cut rectangles of paper-backed fusible transfer web 1" wide by 1" longer than the buttonholes. Center them over the wrong side of the buttonhole openings with the web

side down. Fuse, remove the paper backings, then trim the web out of the openings. (Fig. 7-17)

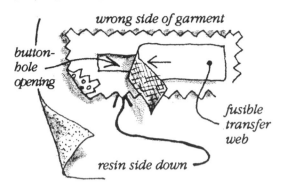

Fig. 7-17: *Pull interfacing to wrong side of garment. Finger-press and fuse. Center transfer web over opening and press lightly.*

6. To make the buttonhole lips, cut a 1"-wide strip of fabric twice the length of each buttonhole plus 2". Fold the strips in half lengthwise with wrong sides together. Serge-finish the folds with a satin-length, balanced, 3-thread or rolled-edge stitch. This serging is decorative, so test for the most attractive type and width of stitch for your fabric and pattern. Test different thread types as well.

7. Cut each strip in half and butt the serged edges together. Bartack them together at each end to form the buttonhole lips. The bartacks should not show in the finished buttonholes.

8. From the right side, center the buttonhole openings over the right side of the lips and fuse them in place, using a press cloth to prevent shine. (Fig. 7-18)

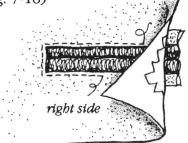

right side

Fig. 7-18: *Center buttonhole over lips. Fuse in place and top-stitch.*

9. Top-stitch around the boxes, just outside the edges.

10. Fuse the facing to the back side of the buttonholes.

Project: Three-Button Belt

Easy serge-bound buttonholes provide the decorative detail on this *Ultrasuede* belt. It's adjustable by using one, two, or all three buttonholes. (Fig. 7-19)

Fig. 7-19: *Adjustable belt has three serge-bound buttonholes.*

Stitch: 3-thread
Stitch length: Short
Stitch width: Narrow to medium
Thread: Contrasting color
    Needle: All-purpose or serger
    Upper looper: Woolly nylon
    Lower looper: Woolly nylon
Tension: balanced
Needle: Size 11/75
Fabric: 34" by 4" strip *Ultrasuede* for belt (or adjust for your waist measurement plus 7"—see Note below); 12" by 1" strip lightweight broadcloth or other woven for buttonhole lips
Notions: 2" by 34" (see Note below) stiff fusible interfacing for belt backing; 16" by 2" strip lightweight nonwoven fusible interfacing for buttonholes; 16" by 1" strip paper-backed fusible web for six buttonhole windows; three 1" buttons

N **Note:** The belt measurements fit a size 27" to 32-1/2" waist. To alter, add to or subtract from the length of both the *Ultrasuede* strip and the stiff fusible interfacing. Use your waist measurement plus 7".

1. Cut the long strip of *Ultrasuede* in half lengthwise. Interface one strip for the top of the belt.

2. Starting 1/2" from one end, mark three 1-1/4" horizontal buttonholes 1-1/2" apart on the wrong side of each strip.

3. Place a 2-1/4" by 2" rectangle of fusible interfacing over the right side of each buttonhole with the resin side up. From the wrong side, straight-stitch buttonhole rectangles over the markings.

4. Cut the buttonholes open, clipping to the corners. Turn the interfacing to the wrong side, finger-pressing, then fusing.

5. Cut three 2-1/4" by 1" rectangles of transfer web. Center and fuse them over the buttonholes. Remove the paper backings and trim out the openings.

6. Fold the strip of broadcloth in half lengthwise and serge-finish the edge with a narrow satin stitch.

7. Cut six 2" sections from the serged strip. Form three sets of buttonhole lips by butting the serged edges together and bartacking very near both ends.

8. From the right side, center the belt top over the right side of the lips and fuse in place using a press cloth. Top-stitch around the boxes on the outside of the buttonholes. Fuse the wrong side of the under belt to the back of the buttonholes.

9. With wrong sides together, serge around all sides of the belt with a narrow satin stitch to match the buttonhole lips.

10. Attach the buttons to match the buttonholes.

Lesson 34. Serged Elastic Button Loops

For a baby garment or a delicate feminine effect, serge-finish an edge with elastic thread in the lower looper. Then simply pull out elastic button loops at desired intervals for a quick and easy decorative closure.

1. Prepare your serger with decorative thread in the upper looper, elastic thread in the lower looper, and all-purpose or serger thread in the needle.

2. Adjust for a short, medium- to wide-width stitch. We prefer the 3-thread, although a 4-thread overedge stitch looks fine as well. Balance the tension with the upper looper thread slightly wrapping the edge. This makes the elastic invisible from the top side.

S **Special Tip:** You might have to play with the lower looper (elastic thread) tension to get it adjusted properly because the thread stretches so easily. Even then, the lower looper thread loops probably will not be precisely even due to the nature of the elastic thread. If you cannot loosen the lower looper tension enough, take the elastic thread out of the tension dial. Apply a little more tension by wrapping it around the differential-feed lever or first thread guide.

3. After testing the stitch, serge-finish one side of the closure.

4. Use pins to mark equidistant button placements along the outer edge of the serged elastic loops. With a fine crochet hook or tapestry needle, pull the elastic thread at each mark to form small, even loops. (Fig. 7-20) Pulling the elastic thread narrows and tightens the decorative edge slightly and anchors the loops.

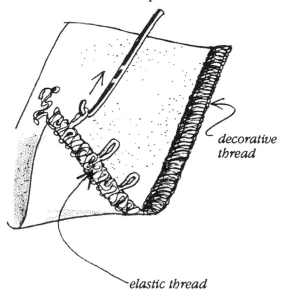

Fig. 7-20: Serge-finish one edge with elastic thread in lower looper. Pull elastic to form loops.

5. Change to all-purpose or serger thread in the lower looper and re-adjust the stitch to match the width and appearance of the decorative serging on the looped edge (now narrower than originally serged because you have pulled the loops).

6. Serge-finish the opposite closure edge. Sew small buttons in the middle of the row of stitching to match the elastic loop placements.

Project: Serge-finished Collar

Select a pretty place mat or dresser scarf for this simple collar. Use serged elastic button loops for the closure. Position the closure on either the front or back of the collar. (Fig. 7-21)

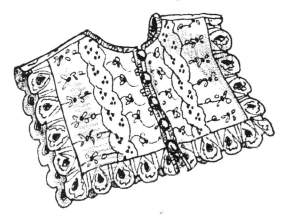

Fig. 7-21: Place-mat collar with serged elastic button-loop closure.

Stitch: 3-thread
Stitch length: Short
Stitch width: Wide
Thread: Matching color
    Needle: All-purpose or serger
    Upper looper: Woolly nylon
    Lower looper: Elastic thread for looped closure; all-purpose or serger thread for serge-finishing

Tension: Balanced
Needle: Size 11/75
Fabric: One place mat or dresser scarf with crocheted edging, eyelet, Battenburg lace, or other decorative detailing
Notions: Five or more 7/16" ball buttons

1. Using a basic jewel neckline pattern, cut the neckline and shoulder edges for the front and back collar. (Fig. 7-22) Trim 1/2" of the seam allowance from the neckline. Cut along the center front or back for the collar opening.

2. Serge-seam the shoulders with a medium-length, balanced stitch.

3. Adjust your serger for serged elastic button loops. Serge-finish the right front or the right back.

4. Pull the elastic thread at equidistant intervals to form button loops. The number of loops and their spacing depends on the depth of your collar and the desired effect.

5. Rethread the lower looper and readjust for matching decorative stitching. Serge-finish the other side of the opening.

6. Fold 1/8" of the neckline to the wrong side and serge-finish with the same stitch adjustment as in step 5. Thread the chain tails back through the stitches to secure.

7. Attach buttons to match the loop placements.

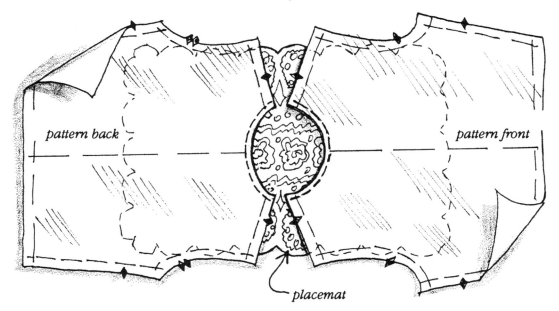

pattern back

pattern front

placemat

Fig. 7-22: *Cut collar front and back from place mat or dresser scarf.*

8. Expanding Your Artistic Possibilities

- **Lesson 35. Serger Chain Art**
- **Lesson 36. Serged Appliqué**
- **Lesson 37. Serger Cutwork**
- **Lesson 38. Embellished Fabric**

In previous chapters, we discussed traditional decorative seaming, edge-finishing, and special techniques. We also included a number of brand-new serger applications that we discovered during our research for this book. Serge-bound seams and edges, clear elastic trim and piping, and serged elastic button loops are some notable examples.

For this final chapter, we will cover creative possibilities that usually aren't associated with serger sewing. Although we had done some work with serger chain, appliqué, cutwork, and fabric embellishment in the past (see our two books, *Distinctive Serger Gifts & Crafts* and *Simply Serge Any Fabric*), we felt that we had barely begun to explore these areas.

Having the time to test and develop more ideas was the major factor limiting our research. Yet artistic possibilities seem endless, including combinations of decorative techniques and unusual applications for existing techniques, as well as the continual introduction of new products and technology. What we have included in these last four lessons is merely a starting point—for us and, we hope, for you—to push the serger to its creative limits.

Lesson 35. Serger Chain Art

Originally used for professional-looking button and belt loops, serger chain art has now become an exciting medium for artistic expression in both craft and dressmaking projects. With the wide array of decorative threads and yarns available for serger use, possibilities abound for interesting chain projects. And the speedy serger can make yards and yards of chain in minimal time.

Now we've begun to explore serger-chain tassels, fringe, cording, and jewelry. (Fig. 8-1) Although some of these projects are more craft-oriented, others can be used to ornament your latest fashion garments. And you won't have to worry about not finding the perfect color or texture—you can coordinate it yourself.

Fig. 8-1: *Artistic uses for serger chain include tassels, fringe, cording, and jewelry.*

1. To make a conventional serger chain, set your machine for a 3-thread rolled edge.

2. Put the thread, yarn, or ribbon you want to feature in the upper looper. This thread will be the most visible in the chain. Anything you can serge with is possible. Try ribbon floss, fine yarn, and a wide variety of decorative threads.

3. Thread the needle with a lightweight matching or monofilament nylon thread. This thread will be the least visible in the chain. For variety,

test other lightweight threads. Fine metallic thread adds a touch of sparkle, while top-stitching thread changes the texture or color.

4. Use woolly or monofilament nylon in the lower looper for the tightest rolled-edge stitch and the firmest chain. Tighten the lower looper tension as much as possible when using shiny thread, such as rayon, in the upper looper.

S **Special Tip:** You may find it impossible to form a tightly rolled edge with a slippery thread in the upper looper. Try instead making a flatter chain by tightening the upper looper tension, too, for a more balanced stitch.

5. Adjust your stitch length and tensions for the thread you're using. If you have difficulty starting because of your decorative thread, serge a few inches on fabric, then chain off. (Fig. 8-2) When using heavy thread such as pearl cotton or crochet thread,

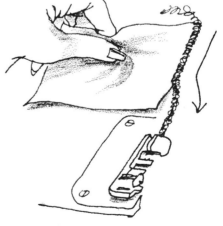

Fig. 8-2: *To begin, serge a few inches on fabric, then chain off.*

start with a stitch length of 3mm and shorten it gradually to get the most attractive stitch formation. If the stitch length is too short, the thread can jam at the presser foot.

6. Hold the thread taut behind the presser foot for a more uniform chain. If there are skipped stitches in the chain, try switching to a size 14/90 needle. Also try loosening the tensions a small amount, one at a time. First adjust the lower looper, then the upper looper, and finally the needle.

Test unusual serger chain-stitching options. Vary the stitch size and tensions. Try serging over one or more strands of heavy filler thread. (Place the filler thread over the front and under the back of the presser foot, between the needle and knives.) Or, for more options, substitute fine wire for the filler thread. (We'll use fine wire later in this lesson to wrap a tassel.) Puffed serged braid (page 105) is actually a serger-chain variation made with balanced tension and a thicker filler.

Thread-chain cording

Make cording from serger chain by using the bobbin winder on your sewing machine.

1. Knot one or more long strands of serger chain through a hole in the bobbin. (Fig. 8-3) The strand(s) should be twice as long as the desired cording length. The length of the strand is limited by the length of your arms, unless you have one person run the machine while another holds the chain.

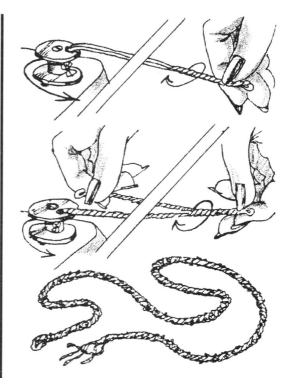

Fig. 8-3: *Attach strands to bobbin and wind. Hold at halfway point and wind outer half back onto bobbin half.*

2. Hold the free end of the serger chain securely. Wind the bobbin until the strands are firmly twisted.

3. Before removing the cording from the bobbin, hold the twisted strands at the halfway point with your other hand. The cording will automatically twist back on itself. Pull the cording until the twisting is uniform.

Serger-chain cording may be used for decorative accents (such as edge trimming or couching), accessory items (necklaces or belts), or home decoration (pillow trims and drapery tie-backs).

Special Tip: For heavy cording that is too thick to tie to a bobbin, have one person hold one end of the strand(s) while another person does the twisting. Or tie one end to a doorknob on a closed door and twist from the free end.

Thread-chain fringe

Make your own decorative fringe from serger chain. For 1" fringe, cut a piece of tear-away stabilizer 3" wide by the desired length. Fold it length-wise into a 1" width (3 layers). Vary the width of the stabilizer to change the length of the fringe. Wrap the serger chain loosely around the stabilizer. With a medium- to wide-width satin balanced stitch, serge along one edge with the same decorative thread in the upper looper. (Fig. 8-4) Dab seam sealant on the chains on the

other edge so they won't unravel, allow them to dry, and cut. Tear away the stabilizer. Top-stitch the fringe to your project through the upper row of stitching.

Thread-chain tassels

Make tassels from any size serger chain. (Fig. 8-5) For a delicate tassel, use rayon, lingerie, or fine metallic thread. Try pearl cotton, pearl rayon, or crochet thread for a heavier tassel. Rayon thread will make the smoothest chain. Serge at least six yards of chain for one tassel. Smaller chain will require more strands for a fuller appearance.

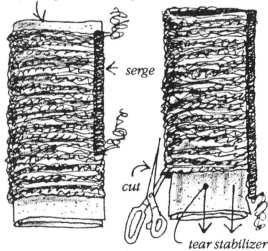

tear-away stabilizer layers

serge

cut

tear stabilizer

Fig. 8-4: Wrap chain around stabilizer. Serge upper edge and cut lower edge. Tear away stabilizer for finished fringe.

Fig. 8-5: Make tassels from any size serger chain.

1. Loosely wind the chain over a firm piece of cardboard cut to the length of your tassel. The more chain that is wrapped, the fuller the tassel. Do not stretch the chain while winding.

2. Cut a 6" strand of chain for the tassel hanger. Tie the chains together at one end of the cardboard, as shown. (Fig. 8-6) Dab seam sealant

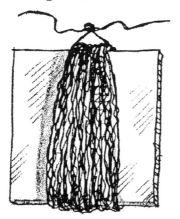

Fig. 8-6: Tie chain together at one end of cardboard.

on the chains on the opposite end of the cardboard so they won't unravel. Allow them to dry before cutting.

3. About 3/4" below the tied ends, form a loop of chain and wrap over it. After you have completed the wrapping, thread the chain ends through the loop and pull to secure. (Fig. 8-7) Hide the ends under the edge of the wrapping.

 Optional: Serge an 8" chain strand over fine wire. Wrap the tassel, twist the ends together, and tuck them under the wrapping.

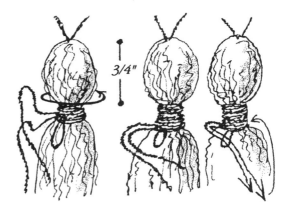

Fig. 8-7: Form thread-chain loop and wrap over it. Pull ends through loop to secure. Tuck tails under wrapping.

Project: Double-wrapped Tassel

Make two tassels to finish the ends of the table runner in Lesson 17, page 91. (Fig. 8-8) Test matching metallic

Fig. 8-8: Simple thread chain tassels feature two wrappings. Attach to table runner from Lesson 17.

yarn in a chain before using it for the tassels. If you find that it is too wiry, opt for a matching color of softer heavy rayon thread.

Stitch: 3-thread
Stitch length: Short
Stitch width: Narrow
Thread: Matching color
    Needle: All-purpose or serger
    Upper looper: Decorative thread
    Lower looper: Woolly nylon
Tension: Rolled edge
Needle: Size 11/75
Notions: 16" of 24-gauge fine, flexible wire (such as bead wire, purchased at a craft store); a small amount of yarn in a matching color (enough to form two 3/4" balls); cardboard

1. Serge 22 yards of chain for two tassels. With the same serger adjustments and decorative thread, carefully serge over the wire.

2. Cut off 48" of chain and section it into four 12" pieces.

3. For each tassel, loosely wrap half the long chain around a 5" piece of cardboard. Tie the chains together at one side of the cardboard using one of the shorter chains. See Figure 8-6.

4. Dab seam sealant on the thread chains at the opposite end so they won't unravel. Allow them to dry, then cut the ends evenly.

5. With the other 12" chains, wrap each tassel together tightly about 3/4" from the top. Secure the ends by placing them through the loop, as shown in step 3 of the thread-chain tassel instructions on page 153.

6. Wind the matching yarn into balls and insert in each tassel between the thread-chain strands close to the wrapped sections.

7. With 8" of the wire, wrap each tassel tightly, enclosing and securing the yarn ball. Insert the wire ends under the wrapped edges. Adjust the thread chains to cover the yarn. (Fig. 8-9) (Or use two additional 12" chains to wrap the tassels as in step 5 above.)

Twist wire ends together and tuck under.

Fig. 8-9: *Use chain serged over fine wire to wrap tassel.*

8. Hand-tack the tassels to each end of the table runner, covering the trim joints.

Lesson 36.
Serged Appliqué

Appliqué is one of our favorite embellishments because it offers so many options for creativity. You can use it to add texture, color, and a three-dimensional effect to any fabric. Fashion your own design to adorn your latest garments, sweaters, accessories, or home decoration projects.

In the past, we've worked with flat and 3-D appliqué. We've also tried padded appliqué. Just about any serged edge-finish or trim can be used. Other techniques such as serger lace and serging over sequins, beads, or pearls adapt well to appliqué. Let your creativity guide you.

Serge-finish the edges of the pieces you plan to appliqué. A satin rolled-edge stitch is the most common for edge finishing, but any serged edge is possible.

Apply the appliqué pieces to your fabric by top-stitching all of the edges flat, top-stitching only part of the edges (for a raised or 3-D appliqué), or attaching them by hand-tacking, fusing, or fabric painting. (Fig. 8-10)

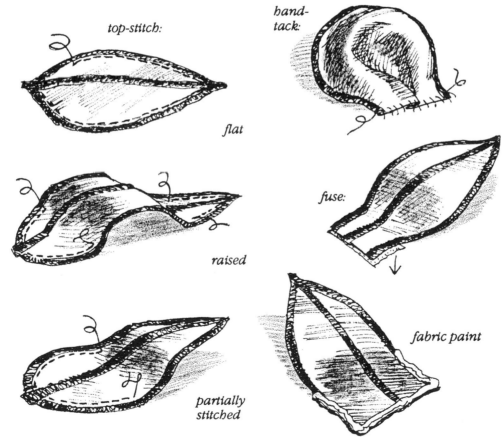

top-stitch:

flat

hand-tack:

raised

fuse:

partially stitched

fabric paint

Fig. 8-10: *Appliqué serge-finished pieces to project fabric.*

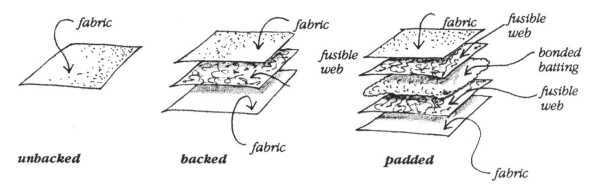

unbacked   *backed*   *padded*

Fig. 8-11: *Appliqués can be cut from unbacked, backed, or padded fabric.*

Appliqués may be unbacked, backed, or padded. (Fig. 8-11) Unbacked appliqués are usually applied flat to the project fabric with the under side of the appliqué fabric hidden. Make backed appliqués simply by sandwiching a layer of fusible transfer web between two layers of fabric (right sides out) so that both sides of the appliqué will appear finished when they are applied by the raised or 3-D methods.

Make padded appliqués by sandwiching bonded batting between two layers of fusible transfer web. Then fuse the batting and web between two layers of fabric, with the web against the wrong side of the fabric. Padded appliqués are most often applied raised or 3-D, in the same manner as unpadded, backed appliqués.

Project: Appliquéd Evening Bag

Serged appliqué adorns this unique evening bag. Make the strap by cording thread chain, then top the bag with the pearl-trimmed organza flower made in Lesson 28 (page 129). (Fig. 8-12)

Fig. 8-12: *Appliquéd evening bag with cording strap, satin leaves, and flower from Lesson 28.*

Stitch: 3-thread for appliqué; 3-thread or 4-thread overedge for serge-seaming

Stitch length: Short for appliqué; medium for serge-seaming

Stitch width: Narrow for appliqué; widest for serge-seaming

Thread: Matching color
  Needle(s): All-purpose or serger
  Upper looper: Rayon or other decorative for appliqué; all-purpose or serger for serge-seaming
  Lower looper: Woolly nylon for appliqué; all-purpose or serger for serge-seaming

Tension: Rolled edge for appliqué; balanced for serge-seaming

Needle(s): Size 11/75

Fabric: 1/2 yard taffeta for outer bag; 1/2 yard matching lining fabric for bag lining; 1/6 yard matching satin for appliquéd leaves

Notions: 10" polyester fleece; 10" heavy fusible interfacing; 6" by 12" piece paper-backed fusible web; one spool matching ribbon floss; one large snap

1. Cut 10" by 18" rectangles from the taffeta, lining, fleece, and interfacing. Fuse the interfacing to the fleece.

2. From the ribbon floss, make one yard of thread-chain cording following the instructions on page 151.

3. Match the ends of the cording to the cut edges of the right side of the lining 6-1/2" from the top on both sides. (Fig. 8-13) With the right sides of the taffeta and lining together, place the fleece on top of the taffeta.

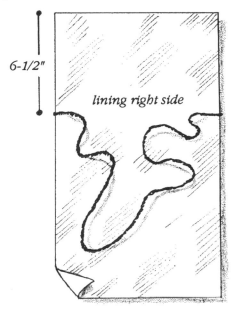

6-1/2"

lining right side

Fig. 8-13: *Position cording on top of lining.*

4. Serge-seam the four sides of the bag, leaving an opening at the lower edge for turning and being careful to catch only the cording ends in the serging. Secure the cording in the seam by straight-stitching again over the cording with a short stitch length.

5. Turn the bag to the right side and fold the opening allowances to the inside. Press carefully. Edge-stitch across the lower edge, closing the opening.

6. At the lower edge, fold 4-1/2" to the wrong side to form the bag. From the right side of the bag, edge-stitch the three unfolded edges. (Fig. 8-14)

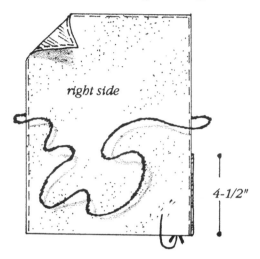

Fig. 8-14: Fold lower edge to form pocket. Edge-stitch.

7. Fold the upper edge down even with the cording placement, forming the flap. Press lightly.

8. To make the leaf appliqué, fuse the transfer web to the back of the satin fabric. Remove the paper backing and fuse the other side to the wrong side of a matching rectangle of the satin. Using the grid as a pattern, cut one large leaf and one small leaf set from the fused satin. (Fig. 8-15)

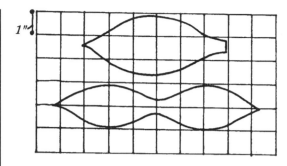

Fig. 8-15: Pattern for large leaf and small leaf set.

9. With your serger adjusted for appliqué sewing (see specifications on page 157), fold the leaves in half lengthwise and serge the folded edge, forming the leaf ribs. (Fig. 8-16) Pull the leaves flat and serge-finish all leaf edges.

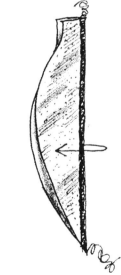

Fig. 8-16: Fold leaf in half and serge fold with satin rolled edge.

10. Place the large leaf on the bag flap, raising the center rib three-dimensionally. Top-stitch both sides, starting and ending about 1-1/2" from the leaf ends.

11. Pin a tuck in the middle of the smaller leaf set and place it over the larger leaf, as shown. (Fig. 8-17) Top-stitch both leaves as you did the larger one. Straight-stitch across the bottom of all three leaves to secure.

Fig. 8-17: Appliqué leaves to bag flap.

12. Attach the flower made in Lesson 28 over the center of the leaves. Hand-sew the large snap, securing the flap to the top of the bag.

Lesson 37.
Serger Cutwork

Our first introduction to serger cutwork was when Sue Green wrote about it for our *Serger Update* newsletter in early 1988. Although it was a fascinating technique, it took considerable skill and patience to serge-finish the inner edge of small holes cut in a piece of fabric. (Fig. 8-18)

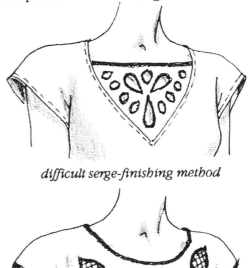

difficult serge-finishing method

easy water-soluble stabilizer method

Fig. 8-18: Serger cutwork options.

Then we discovered an interesting new product—water-soluble stabilizer—and Naomi started experimenting. The results were a speedy combination of sewing and serging that created an interesting new appliquéd cutwork. (Fig. 8-18)

This newer method works equally well for garments, table linens, and craft projects. The cutwork appliqué must be applied to a washable fabric, because the washable stabilizer has to be dissolved in water to complete the project.

Serging over the stabilizer gives stitches a stiff, starched effect. Test various threads and stitch types for the desired effect. For example, woolly nylon in a satin rolled edge creates a stiff design. With a longer balanced stitch, it gives a softer appearance.

1. With a water-soluble pen, draw a cutwork design outline on the project fabric. (Fig. 8-19)

2. Cut a piece of water-soluble stabilizer at least 1" larger than the design on all sides.

3. Draw serging guidelines onto the stabilizer. (Fig. 8-19) For more durability, draw the guidelines close together and limit the size of the appliqué. Plan straight rows of serging for your first project, because serging a curved fold can by tricky.

4. Fold the stabilizer on the guidelines and serge over the folds with a stitch adjustment you have previously tested. (Don't worry if you cut the stabilizer.)

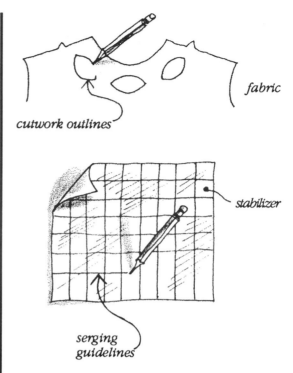

Fig. 8-19: *Draw cutwork outlines on fabric and serging guidelines on water-soluble stabilizer.*

5. Pull the stabilizer flat, stretching it over the outline on the right side of the base fabric. Pin it in place. (Fig. 8-20) Be sure the serged stitches extend past the design outline on all sides.

6. With matching thread and a narrow, satin stitch, zigzag the stabilizer to the fabric following the design outline.

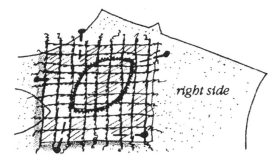

Fig. 8-20: *Pin serged stabilizer over cutwork outline. Zigzag to fabric.*

7. Trim the stabilizer close to the outside of the zigzag stitch. Be careful not to cut the zigzag stitch or the fabric. (Fig. 8-21)

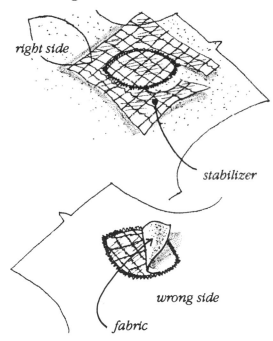

right side

stabilizer

wrong side

fabric

Fig. 8-21: *Trim stabilizer outside zigzag on front. Trim fabric inside zigzag on back.*

8. Carefully trim away the fabric from behind the stabilizer appliqué. To finish and secure the cutwork, stitch over the original zigzagging from the right side. Use a narrow, satin zigzag stitch just a little wider than the original stitching in step 6.

9. Submerge the cutwork appliqué in water to remove the stabilizer. Allow it to air dry, or press it dry between two layers of press cloth.

Project: Tuck-and-Roll Tablecloth with Cutwork

Decorate the tuck-and-roll tablecloth from Lesson 6 (page 64) with a cutwork design. (Fig. 8-22) Use the cutwork motif on one or more corners of the project.

Fig. 8-22: *Tuck-and-roll tablecloth from Lesson 6 with appliquéd cutwork.*

Stitch: 3-thread
Stitch length: Short (2mm)
Stitch width: Narrow
Thread: Matching color
    Needle: All-purpose or serger
    Upper looper: All-purpose or
      serger
    Lower looper: All-purpose or
      serger
Tension: Flatlock
Needle: Size 11/75
Notions: One 6" by 6" square
    water-soluble stabilizer; air-
    erasable or washable marker

1. Draw a 4" oval in the corner of the tablecloth using a disappearing marker.

2. Serge the stabilizer with rows of stitching in a criss-crossed design of your choice. Extend the rows of serging to fill the stabilizer square.

3. Center the serged stabilizer over the oval. Stretch it and pin the edges. Zigzag around the oval with a short, narrow stitch.

4. Carefully cut away the serged stabilizer outside the oval, next to the zigzag stitching. On the back, trim the fabric from underneath the stabilizer inside the oval.

5. With a slightly wider satin-length zigzag, stitch over the original zigzagging.

6. Soak the design in water to remove the stabilizer. Let dry, or carefully press between two press cloths.

Lesson 38. Embellished Fabric

Although there is a difference between actually constructing yardage on your serger and ornamenting fabric by adding serged stitches and detail, we group them together here.

Constructing fabric

Using a serger to construct patchwork fabric has been explored in detail by many sewing professionals. Myriad patchwork designs are possible, and they can be constructed more quickly than with a sewing machine because of the serger's faster stitching.

Another option for constructing decorative fabric on your serger is to mix fabric types, textures, or colors to complement the design of your garment. The method of seaming the elements together can be decorative as well. Exposed seams of any type or color are an option.

Inserts are yet another way to create unusual fabric for your project. Strips of synthetic suede or leather can be placed strategically in the middle of your fashion fabric. Tapestry insets add a hand-detailed effect. Or a lighter-weight fabric strip can be serge-gathered on both long edges and inserted as a decorative detail. (Fig. 8-23)

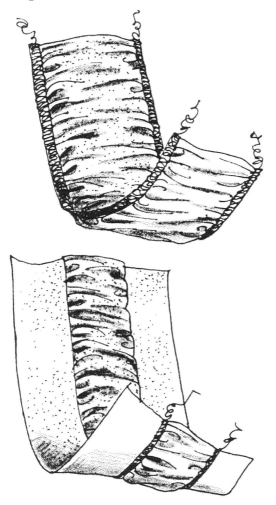

Fig. 8-23: *Serge-gather fabric strip and inset on yardage.*

Ornamenting fabric

Heirloom serging (a replication of French hand-sewing) was an early example of serger-embellished fabric. Delicate rows of pintucks, lace inserts, and rolled edges are quickly applied to a fabric such as batiste, organdy, or handkerchief linen. An art in itself, beautiful heirloom serging has been featured extensively in books and articles.

We want to take the art of ornamenting fabric one step further. You don't have to use dainty stitches on lightweight woven fabrics in straight rows in order to embellish your fabric. Consider all of your ornamental serging possibilities. Most edge-finishes also can be serged over folds, so you have the option of placing stitches anywhere on your fabric—and in any direction.

Try diagonal or vertical rows of corded rolled edges, perhaps to accent a stripe in the fabric. Test parallel rows of wide, balanced, satin serging to duplicate current designer fabrics. (Or try prepleating a fabric with a *Perfect Pleater* device and serge-finishing each tuck.) Consider serging with uneven spacing, sporadi-

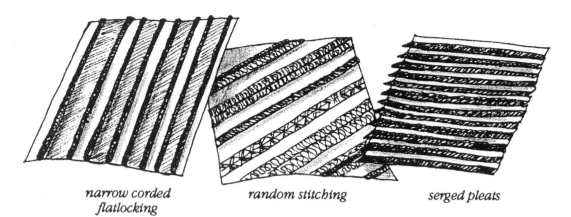

narrow corded
flatlocking

random stitching

serged pleats

Fig. 8-24: Ornament fabrics with corded flatlocking on stripes, random diagonal stitches, or narrow serged pleats.

cally placed stitching, or combinations of techniques. (Fig. 8-24)

Experiment with all fabric types and any decorative thread. Test ideas from ready-to-wear. Let your imagination soar. We include a few test results here, but these are only the beginning. There's plenty of room for innovation in serger sewing. Have fun, experiment, and let us know what you discover.

Chain-loop serging—Our first idea for this technique was to serge on and off a fold or edge, using a satin rolled edge and leaving thread-chain loops at intervals along the stitching. We serged for a distance and then chained off the fabric. To form a loop, we raised the presser foot, anchored the needle right where the chain left the fabric, and began serging again.

Although we achieved an interesting effect (Fig. 8-25), the method was

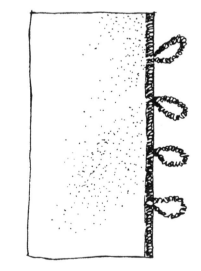

Fig. 8-25: Serge on and off fabric for chain-loop detail.

slow and tedious. Naomi discovered a faster, more random effect by serging with the presser foot up the entire time. She was able to chain off and on easily. Leave the chain in loops or cut it at varying lengths. We've used this technique for the scarf project at the end of this chapter.

Flatlocked patches—With a heavier thread such as pearl rayon in the upper looper, create short patches of flatlocking in the middle of your fabric, leaving thread tails at each end. Tie beads onto the tails for an added ornamental touch. (Fig. 8-26) Mark the placement of your flatlocked patches or apply them randomly. Fold along the placement line. Remove the stitches from the stitch finger and pull out about 3" of un-chained thread. Raise the presser foot and anchor the needle at the end of the placement line.

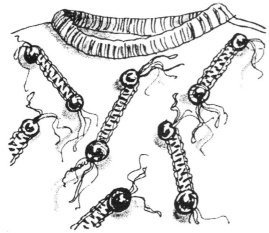

Fig. 8-26: *Flatlock random patches on fabric. Tie beads on tails.*

Flatlock the patch, lift the presser foot, and pull the threads away from the serging. Do not chain off. Knot the threads at each end or attach beads to secure the stitching.

Try decorative patches using a rolled-edge or narrow balanced stitch. Or try chaining on and off the fabric for a different effect.

Finger tensioning—We used finger tensioning to gather lightweight fabric in Lesson 23 (page 111). It also can be used to vary the look of your decorative stitching.

First we tried applying tension on the looper threads, but with little success. We then went back to the needle thread (used for tension gathering). By putting tension on the needle thread of a narrow flatlock at equal intervals, we achieved a scalloped flatlocked effect. (Fig. 8-27)

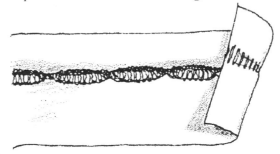

Fig. 8-27: *Use finger tensioning for scalloped flatlock.*

Don't be afraid to try other methods for varying your decorative stitch at intervals during your serging.

Charted needlework variation— Those serger enthusiasts who have done charted needlework on the sewing machine may want to explore its application for the serger.

As long as the needle fits between the edge of the bed and the serger needle (and the looper can pass over it), you can serge charted needlework. Tammy was able to serge easily over a size 8 knitting needle using a BL4-738 model.

To make loops on a fold of fabric, remove the presser foot and disengage the knife. Your stitch adjustment should be similar to a reversible-edge binding stitch (page 69). Hold a knitting needle along the edge of your serger's bed to the right of the serger needle. Butt a fold of fabric up against the left side of the knitting needle. Serge slowly, catching the fold with the serged stitching. (Fig. 8-28)

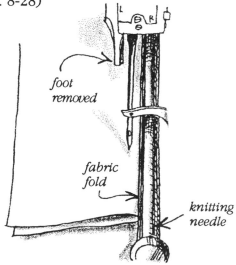

foot removed

fabric fold

knitting needle

Fig. 8-28: *Serge over knitting needle, catching looped stitches in fold of fabric.*

 Note: Test by hand first to be certain the stitch is adjusted correctly and that the needle and looper clear the knitting needle.

Without removing the knitting needle from the stitching, fold again near the first row and repeat the instructions above using a second needle. (Because the knitting needle can be held securely against the edge of the bed, serging over charted needles can be easier for a beginner than sewing over them.)

After serging over two large needles with woolly nylon in the loopers, we made a fringed trim by cutting the center of the loop rows. (Fig. 8-29)

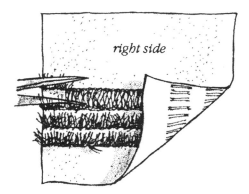

right side

Fig. 8-29: *Fringe trim by cutting center of loops. Apply seam sealant or fusible interfacing to ladder stitches on back.*

To secure the stitches, run seam sealant along the rows of stitches on the back of the fabric, or neatly fuse them in place with fusible interfacing.

We know there are many more possibilities for serging raised stitches over needles, so put your imagination to work.

Project: Embellished Chiffon Scarf

Embellish a fashionable 2-yard chiffon scarf with random decorative serging for an attention-getting accessory. (Fig. 8-30)

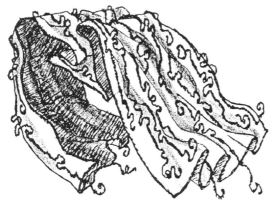

Fig. 8-30: *Free-form embellishment on long chiffon scarf.*

Stitch: 2- or 3-thread
Stitch length: Short (1mm to 2mm)
Stitch width: Narrow
Thread: Contrasting color
   Needle: All-purpose or serger
   Upper looper: Woolly nylon
   Lower looper: Woolly nylon
Tension: Rolled edge
Needle: Size 11/75
Fabric: 2 yards chiffon
Notions: Optional—ornamental
   beads to tie on thread-chain tails

1. Cut a piece of chiffon the length of the fabric by 18" wide. Finish all four sides with a rolled edge.

2. Using the techniques described on page 164 under chain-loop serging, fill the scarf with random rows of decorative serging.

3. Leave the chain loops or clip them apart at varying lengths. Tie on ornamental beads if desired.

baby lock *History*

In 1967, the Juki Company, Incorporated, of Tokyo, Japan, developed the first household serger. Exceptionally knowledgeable about the large, high-speed industrial overlock machines used in factory production, they conceived of these machines as the "parent" of today's home sergers. After designing and producing a precise-copy miniature overlock for home use, they called it a "baby" overlock, or *baby lock*.

The *baby lock* gained overnight acceptance among Japanese consumers, who recognized the tremendous advantages of serger methods for their home sewing. Based on the *baby lock*'s ever-growing popularity, Juki soon sought foreign marketing opportunities.

The first U.S. importer of *baby locks* was a distributor of industrial machines for the garment industry. The majority of early *baby lock* sales were to tailors, alteration shops, and small cottage industry. Garment factory workers also purchased sergers so they could use professional factory methods in their home-sewing projects.

From the beginning, Tacony Corporation, with great success, marketed the *baby lock* through its industrial machine division. It later gained exclusive distribution rights for the *baby lock* in the U.S. market and first introduced the new concept of serger sewing at an American Home Economics Association convention. Tacony was the first to offer dealer training seminars on the operation, sales, and repair of sergers, and it pioneered the use of specially trained home economists to educate both dealers and consumers on serger sewing techniques.

Consumers responded. The *baby lock*'s advantages dovetailed perfectly with the changing American lifestyle. As an increasing number of women joined the work force, serger sewing offered them both the speed they needed to fit home sewing into their busy schedules and the professional-quality results they required for their career wardrobes.

Since the serger's introduction, Tacony has continually upgraded its available models by adding options such as differential feed and a variety of stitch formations. The company also added convenience features like automatic needle and looper threaders and electronic foot controls.

Sergers have generated a renewal of interest and excitement in home sewing. Every major sewing machine company now markets overlock machines under its own brand name, confirming Tacony's early vision of the serger's potential popularity.

Glossary of Serging Terms

All-purpose or serger thread—All-purpose thread usually means cotton-covered polyester wound parallel on conventional spools. Standard serger thread has the same fiber content but is lighter in weight than all-purpose thread and is cross-wound on cones or tubes so that it can feed more easily during higher-speed serger sewing.

Balanced stitch—A serge-finished edge or seam in which the upper- and lower-looper thread tensions are balanced so the threads meet at the edge of the fabric, forming loops.

Binding—A strip of fabric sewn to an edge, then wrapped around it and secured to hide the seam and the raw edge.

Decorative seam (also decorative exposed seam)—Any seam on the outside of a garment or project that enhances design detail.

Decorative thread (also decorative serging or decorative finish)—Any thread other than all-purpose or serger thread, although even a contrasting color of these threads is technically considered decorative. Our favorite decorative threads include woolly nylon, rayon, pearl cotton, silk, buttonhole twist, and metallic. New threads are introduced regularly.

Edge-stitch—A medium-length (10 - 12 stitches/inch) straight stitch on a conventional sewing machine, which is applied near the edge of anything being sewn. Edge-stitching is often used to join two serge-finished layers.

Filler cord—Crochet thread, pearl cotton, or buttonhole twist that simulates piping when serged over with a short (satin) stitch.

Flatlock—A technique by which the needle thread is loose enough to flatten out on top of the fabric, forming decorative loops, when the fabric is pulled apart. The underside will show a ladder effect of evenly spaced double parallel stitches. Used for both seaming and decorative stitching on a folded edge, flatlocking lends many creative possibilities. You can flatlock with a 2-thread overedge stitch without a special adjustment; a 3-thread (and even 4-thread overedge) stitch can be adjusted to flatlock as well.

Heavy thread—Crochet thread, pearl cotton, or buttonhole twist used for serge-gathering or filler-cord in serger piping.

Long stitch—A 4 - 5mm serged stitch length.

Machine baste—A long (6 - 8 stitches/inch) straight stitch on a conventional sewing machine.

Mail order—A growing trend that offers the convenience of at-home catalog shopping. Almost any product is available through mail order, but without the immediate, hands-on selection available at your local fabric store.

Matching thread—Thread the same color as (or that blends as well as possible with) the project fabric.

Medium-length stitch—A 2.5 - 3mm serged stitch length.

Medium-width stitch—A 3.5mm serged stitch width.

Narrow-width stitch—A 2 - 3mm serged stitch width. Used to serge a narrow seam or edge.

Ornamental serging (also decorative serging)—Any serger stitching used to artistically enhance a garment or project. Decorative thread, altered tension, or a combination of serging techniques can be used to create ornamental serging.

Ready-to-wear—Garment available for purchase through retail stores and mail-order outlets.

Rolled edge (finish or seam)—Also called a narrow rolled edge or hem, this stitch is created by altering the tension so that the raw edge rolls to the underside. A short stitch length creates an attractive satin-stitch edge.

Satin stitch (satin length)—A stitch length short enough to allow the thread used to cover the entire fabric over which it is serged. Appropriate for both a balanced stitch or a rolled edge.

Serge-finish—Most often a medium-length, medium-width, and balanced 3- or 4-thread stitch used to finish the edge of one layer during the construction process.

Serge-gather—Several serger techniques are possible for gathering an edge. If your serger has a differential feed, use the 2.0 setting. Another option is to tighten your needle tension and lengthen your stitch. Or simply serge over heavy thread with a balanced stitch, being careful not to catch the heavy thread in the serging. Then, after anchoring one end, pull the heavy thread to gather the edge to any specific length. A fourth option is to loosen the needle tension, serge, and then pull up the needle thread.

Serge-seam—As in serge-finish, a medium-length, medium-width, and balanced 3- or 4-thread stitch, but in this case it's used to seam two layers together.

Short stitch—A 1 - 2mm serged stitch length.

Stitch-in-the-ditch—Stitching directly on top of a previous seam to secure another layer positioned on the underside. Often used for nearly invisible stitching when applying a binding to an edge.

Straight-stitch—A medium-length (10 - 12 stitches/inch) straight stitch on a conventional sewing machine.

Thread chain—The joined loops formed by serging on a properly threaded machine with no fabric.

Top-stitch—A conventional-machine straight stitch (10 - 12 stitches/inch) used to attach one layer (often serged-finished) to another. Top-stitching also can be used as a decorative design detail.

Very wide stitch—A 7.5mm serged stitch width, available on only some serger models.

Wide stitch—A 5mm serged stitch width.

Woolly nylon—One of our favorite decorative threads that became popular with the advent of serger sewing. A crimped nylon thread, it fluffs out to fill in any see-through spaces on a decorative edge.

Zigzag stitch—A basic stitch on a conventional sewing machine that forms a back-and-forth pattern similar to herringbone.

Mail-Order Resources

We recommend that every serger enthusiast develop a special relationship with his or her local dealers and retailers for convenient advice and inspiration, plus the ease of coordinating purchases. However, when specialty items cannot be found locally, or when a home-sewer lives several miles from a sewing retailer, mail-order specialists are a worthwhile option.

The following list will make your search for these resources a breeze. Our list is for reference only and does not carry our endorsement or guarantee. (We have not knowingly included any questionable items or firms.)

S **Special Tip**: To streamline information gathering, be specific even when simply requesting samples or specific product brochures. Let the company know exactly what you are looking for, such as color, fiber, texture, or size.

Risk-free Mail Order

■ **Before you buy**: Read catalog descriptions carefully to make sure the product is what you want. Is there a guarantee? What is the policy for returns?

■ **Placing your order**: Fill out the order form carefully and make a copy of both order and payment for future reference. Never send cash. When ordering by phone, complete the order form first to prevent mistakes. If possible, keep a record of the date of your phone order, as well as the name of the salesperson.

■ **If there is a problem with your order**: Contact the company right away, by phone or by mail. If you contact by phone, be sure to record the time and date of your call, as well as the name of the contact person. Follow up in writing, describing the problem and outlining any solution reached during the phone call. Send copies of your order and payment record. Get a return receipt from the shipper when returning merchandise.

■ **The "30-Day Rule"**: If a delivery date isn't given in a company's materials, the company must ship within 30 days of receiving your order (COD orders excepted), according to the Federal Trade Commission's Mail Order Merchandise Rule. If you place an order using a credit card, your account shouldn't be billed until shipment is made. If you send payment with your order and your order doesn't arrive when promised, you may cancel the order and get a full refund.

A **Authors' note**: In today's volatile business climate, any mail-order source list will change frequently. Please send your comments on any out-of-business notifications or unsatisfactory service to Update Newsletters, 2269 Chestnut #269, San Francisco, CA 94123.

Key to Abbreviations and Symbols:

SASE= self-addressed, stamped (first-class) envelope

L-SASE = large SASE (2-oz. first-class postage)

* = refundable with order

= for information, brochure or catalog

 Note: Check with your postmaster regarding Canadian mail.

Serger Company

Tacony Corporation (*baby lock* and *SergeMate*)
Babylock U.S.A.
P.O. Box 730
St. Louis, MO 63026

Great Serger Notions

Aardvark Adventures, P.O. Box 2449, Livermore, CA 94551, 415/443-2687. Books, beads, buttons, bangles, plus an unusual assortment of related products. Decorative serging thread, including metallics. $1#.

The Bee Lee Company, P.O. Box 36108-B, Dallas, TX 75235. Complete selection of threads, zippers, notions, and trims, including Western styles. Free#.

Bobette Industries, 2401 S. Hill St., Los Angeles, CA 90007-2785, toll-free in CA, 800/237-6462 (orders only). Notions, tools, threads, books, machine parts, and accessories. $1#.

Catherine's, Rt. 6, Box 1227, Lexington, NC 27292, 704/798-1595. Serger threads and more at wholesale prices. Minimum order $35. School quantity discounts. $2 and L-SASE for thread color card.

Clotilde, Inc., 1909 SW First Ave., Ft. Lauderdale, FL 33315, 305/761-8655. Catalog of over 1,200 items, including the *Perfect Pleater*, special serger threads and notions, sewing tools and supplies, and books and videos. $1#.

Custom Zips, P.O. Box 1200, So. Norwalk, CT 06856. Zippers cut to order. $2#.

The Cutting Edge, P.O. Box 76044, St. Peters, MO 63376. Serger notions, including coned threads (all-purpose and decorative), needle threaders, patterns, and carrying cases. L-SASE#.

D & E Distributing, 199 N. El Camino Real #F-242, Encinitas, CA 92024. Decorative threads and yarns, including silk, rayon, and Madeira metallics. L-SASE#.

The Embroidery Stop, 1042 Victory Dr., Yardley, PA 19067. Threads, yarns, and needles. $1#.

Fit For You, 781 Golden Prados Dr., Diamond Bar, CA 91795, 714/861-5021. Sewing notions, serger accessories, videos, and square-dance patterns. L-SASE#.

Home-Sew, Dept. S, Bethlehem, PA 18018. Basic notions, trims, coned serger threads, and tools. Free#.

Jacquart's, 505 E. McLeod, Ironwood, MI 49938, 906/932-1339. Zippers. $1#.

Maryland Trims, P.O. Box 3508, Silver Spring, MD 20901. Laces, sewing notions, and supplies. $1.75#.

Mill End Store, Box 02098, Portland, OR 97202, 503/236-1234. Broad selection of notions, trims, serger threads, and accessories. SASE#.

Nancy's Notions, Ltd., P.O. Box 683, Beaver Dam, WI 53916. Over 300 sewing notions and accessories, serger threads and tools, interfacings and fabrics, and books and videos. Free#.

National Thread & Supply, 695 Red Oak Rd., Stockbridge, GA 30281, 800/847-1001, ext. 1688; in GA, 404/389-9115. Name-brand sewing supplies and notions. Free#.

Newark Dressmaker Supply, P.O. Box 2448, Lehigh Valley, PA 18001, 215/837-7500. Sewing notions, trims, buttons, decorative threads, and serger supplies. Free#.

The Perfect Notion, 566 Hoyt St., Darien, CT 06820, 203/968-1257. Hard-to-find notions and serger threads (including its *ThreadFuse* fusible thread). $1#.

Serge and Sew Notions, 11285 96th Ave. N., Maple Grove, MN 55369, 800/969-7396. Serger threads, books, patterns, furniture, fabrics, and more, priced 20-40% below retail. Free#. Swatch club, $6 for six months.

Serging Ahead, P.O. Box 45, Grandview, MO 64030. Serger threads, books, and patterns. $1#.

Sew-Art International, P.O. Box 550, Bountiful, UT 84010. Decorative threads, notions, and accessories. Free#.

Sew Craft, P.O. Box 1869, Warsaw, IN 46580, 219/269-4046. Books, decorative threads, and notions.

Sew-Fit Co., P.O. Box 565, La Grange, IL 60525, 312/579-3222. Sewing notions and accessories; modular tables for serger/sewing machine setup; books. Free#.

Sewing Emporium, 1087 Third Ave., Chula Vista, CA 92010, 619/420-3490. Hard-to-find sewing notions, sewing machine and serger cabinets and accessories, and serger threads and accessories. $2#.

The Sewing Place, 18870 Cox Ave., Saratoga, CA 95070. Sewing machine and serger needles and feet, plus books by Gale Grigg Hazen. Specify your brand and model if ordering machine accessories. L-SASE#.

The Sewing Workshop, 2010 Balboa St., San Francisco, CA 94121, 415/221-SEWS. Unique designer notions. L-SASE#.

Solo Slide Fasteners, Inc., P.O. Box 528, Stoughton, MA 02072, 800/343-9670. All types and lengths of zippers; other selected notions. Free#.

Speed Stitch, 3113-D Broadpoint Dr., Harbor Heights, FL 33983. Machine art kits and supplies, including all-purpose, decorative, and specialty serging threads, books, and accessories. $3*#.

Thread Discount & Sales, 7105 S. Eastern, Bell Gardens, CA 90201, 213/562-3438. Coned polyester thread. SASE#.

Threads & Things, P.O. Box 83190, San Diego, CA 92138, 619/440-8760. 100% rayon thread. Free#.

Threads West, 422 E. State St., Redlands, CA 92373, 714/793-4405 or 0214. Coned thread, serger parts, and accessories. SASE for free thread color list.

Treadleart, 25834 Narbonne Ave., Suite I, Lomita, CA 90717, 800/327-4222. Books, serging supplies, notions, decorative threads, and creative inspiration. $1.50#.

T-Rific Products Co., P.O. Box 911, Winchester, OR 97495. Coned serger thread. Thread color chart, $1.25.

Two Brothers, 1602 Locust St., St. Louis, MO 63103. Zipper assortment. SASE#.

YLI Corporation, 45 West 300 North, Provo, UT 84601, 800/854-1932 or 801/377-3900. Decorative, specialty, serger, and all-purpose threads, yarns, and ribbons. $1.50#.

Other Publications by the Authors

Serger Update Newsletter, 2269 Chestnut #269, San Francisco, CA 94123. The only periodical devoted entirely to serging news and techniques. Published monthly ($39 annual subscription).

Sewing Update Newsletter (see address above). Newsletter format with tips and ideas from sewing professionals (sister publication to **Serger Update Newsletter**). Sent every other month—$19.50 per year.

Distinctive Serger Gifts & Crafts, Chilton Book Company, 1989. The first book with one-of-a-kind serger projects using ingenious methods and upscale ideas, by Naomi Baker and Tammy Young.

Innovative Serging, Chilton Book Company, 1989. State-of-the-art techniques for overlock sewing by Gail Brown and Tammy Young.

Innovative Sewing, Chilton Book Company, 1990. The newest, best, and fastest sewing techniques by Gail Brown and Tammy Young.

Simply Serge Any Fabric, Chilton Book Company, 1990. Tips and techniques for successfully serging all types of fabric by Naomi Baker and Tammy Young.

The following are **Update Newsletter** booklet publications. They are sold by fabric stores, machine dealers, and mail-order sewing supply companies. Or you can order individual titles for $3.95 each from **Update Newsletters**, 2269 Chestnut #269, San Francisco, CA 94123.

Advanced Serging Techniques, by Naomi Baker, 1988. Never-before-published serger techniques applicable to garment, craft, and decorating projects—serged-scalloped edging, serging padded paper, lace over fishing line and wire, three-dimensional flat and padded appliqué, plus double rolled-edge braid.

Beyond Finishing: Innovative Serging, by Naomi Baker, 1988. A concise, up-to-the-minute report on decorative serging—serged lace, fishline ruffles, tucked and rolled edges, and much more.

Serged Gifts, in Minutes! by Tammy Young, 1988. Charming projects that can be made in an hour or less—like a ruffled hanger, upholstered basket, or firewood carrier (nine total). No pattern purchases are required.

Serging Lingerie, by Naomi Baker, 1988. Learn to serge luxurious lingerie out of both knits and wovens. Edge-finishing and seaming are so easy that you can create beautiful basics or trousseau treasures quickly.

Serging Sweaters, by Naomi Baker, 1988. How to select the right fabrics, make your own pattern from a ready-made favorite, plus pro tips for cutting, seaming, and finishing.

Index

About the Authors

Naomi Baker is a nationally recognized serger authority, who contributes monthly to *Update* newsletters, has authored several *Update* booklets, and has co-authored two previous Chilton books with Tammy Young. A home economics graduate of Iowa State University and former extension agent, she worked for Stretch & Sew for ten years. Naomi also has been an instructor for the Palmer/Pletsch Serger Workshops and provided extensive research for their early publications on serging. She specializes in technique research and development and is well known for her dressmaking skills.

Naomi has a sewing consulting and dressmaking business and appears across the country at special workshops and conventions. She lives and works in Springfield, Oregon, with her husband, three children, dog, huge fabric stash, and an enviable number of sergers and sewing machines.

Tammy Young has combined creativity and practicality in her writing and publishing career. Having worked for several years in the ready-to-wear fashion industry, she is known for her ability to translate retail trends into home-sewing techniques. Tammy is a home economics graduate of Oregon State University and a former extension agent and high school home economics teacher.

Tammy's office is located in San Francisco's Marina District, where she publishes *Update* newsletters and booklets, overseeing all facets of the business, including editing, illustration, layout, printing, and managing all other business details. She makes her home across the Golden Gate Bridge in Sausalito, and when her hectic schedule allows, travels stateside and abroad, frequently picking up trends and ideas for her publications.